Fresh & Tasty

Healthy
cooking

R&R PUBLICATIONS MARKETING PTY LTD

Published by:
R&R Publications Marketing Pty. Ltd
ABN 78 348 105 138
PO Box 254, Carlton North, Victoria 3054 Australia
Phone (61 3) 9381 2199 Fax (61 3) 9381 2689
E-mail: info@randrpublications.com.au
Website: www.randrpublications.com.au
Australia wide toll free: 1800 063 296

©Richard Carroll

Fresh & Tasty Healthy cooking

Publisher: Richard Carroll
Creative Director: Aisling Gallagher
Cover Designer: Lucy Adams
Production Manager: Anthony Carroll
Food Photography: Steve Baxter, Phillip Wilkins, David Munns, Thomas Odulate, Christine
Hanscomb and Frank Wieder
Home Economists: Sara Buenfeld, Emma Patmore, Nancy McDougall, Louise Pickford, Jane
Stevenson, Oded Schwartz, Alison Austin and Jane Lawrie
Food Stylists: Helen Payne, Sue Russell, Sam Scott, Antonia Gaunt and Oded Schwartz
Recipe Development: Terry Farris, Jacqueline Bellefontaine, Becky Johnson, Valerie Barrett, Emma
Patmore, Geri Richards, Pam Mallender and Jan Fullwood
Proofreader: Paul Hassing

Disclaimer: The nutritional information listed with each recipe does not include the nutrient content
of garnishes or any accompaniments not listed in specific quantities in the ingredient list. The
nutritional information for each recipe is an estimate only, and may vary depending on the brand of
ingredients used, and due to natural biological variations in the composition of natural foods such as
meat, fish, fruit and vegetables. The nutritional information was calculated by using the computer
program Foodworks dietary analysis software (version 3.01, Xyris Software Pty. Ltd. Queensland
Australia), and is based on the Australian food composition tables and food manufacturers' data.
Where not specified, ingredients are always analysed as average or medium, not small or large.
The analysis shown is for 100g of the recipe specified.

Includes Index
ISBN 1 74022 444 2
EAN 9 781740 224 444

First Edition Printed September 2004
This Edition Printed January 2006
Computer Typeset in Futura

Printed in Singapore

Cover: Grilled Vegetable Brushetta, Page 22

32

Contents

37

72

Introduction

Nutrition

Food and Health

Our health is affected by what we eat in all sorts of ways and there are some ailments that may require a special diet. This section only gives a general overview of healthy eating. If you have any specific concerns about your health, talk to your doctor.

What's in Food?

Carbohydrates

We need carbohydrates for energy – it really is our daily fuel. Carbohydrates should make up a little more than half our daily calorie intake. Most of it should come from starchy foods like cereals, breads, pasta and potatoes, which are known as complex carbohydrates. These foods supply a steady stream of energy as well as useful vitamins and minerals.

Sugar is an example of a simple carbohydrate, which provides a quick energy boost but no nutrients. Fruits contain natural sugars, and also supply important vitamins and minerals.

Proteins

Every cell in the body – from fingernails to bones and muscles – needs protein for growth, maintenance and repair. Proteins are made up of compounds called amino acids. Anyone who eats a varied diet automatically supplies their body with all the amino acids and protein it needs. But because meat, fish and dairy products are such rich sources of protein, vegetarians and vegans need to ensure they eat a good variety of vegetables, grains, nuts, and pulses to meet their daily requirements.

Fats

If we didn't have fat in our diet, our bodies wouldn't function properly. In fact, to be healthy, up to a third of all the calories we eat should come from fats. Unfortunately, most people in the Australia have a higher proportion of fat than this in their diet, and a high-fat diet can lead to obesity and increased risk of heart disease.

Saturated fats, such as those found in animal fats, are most likely to increase the risk of heart disease by raising blood cholesterol levels. Fatty meats and full-fat dairy products are the main source of saturates in our diets. You don't have to avoid burgers, sausages, cheese, butter and cream completely, just choose lower-fat versions where you can. Buy lean meat and half-fat milk, for example, or just spread your butter a bit more thinly and have a smaller dollop of cream!

The other fats in our diet –

polyunsaturates and monounsaturates – may actually help to lower blood cholesterol. Remember, it's your whole diet that counts. Liquid vegetable oils such as sunflower, grapeseed and olive oil are all high in unsaturated fats. Oil-rich fish such as mackerel, sardines and salmon contain a particular type of polyunsaturated fat (Omega 3) which is also important for a healthy heart. Try to eat oil-rich fish twice a week.

Except for those people who have inherited high cholesterol levels, cholesterol can usually be lowered quite effectively through diet – largely by cutting down on saturated fats and boosting the intake of soluble fibre. Because it binds with cholesterol, soluble fibre helps your body get rid of it as waste, together with undigested fibre. Fruit, vegetables, wholemeal bread, oats and pulses are all good sources of soluble fibre.

Salt

People who eat too much salt are more likely to suffer from high blood pressure. In turn, high blood pressure is a risk factor for heart disease and stroke. In Australia, the recommended daily intake of salt is 5g (about 1 teaspoon), however, the typical person has about 10g. Salt is made up of chlorine and sodium. If you are concerned about your sodium intake, check the nutrition information on food labels.

Eating a Balanced Diet

A balanced diet is one that supplies just the right amount of energy and nutrients for your body's needs. Your body can compensate for times when you eat more or less than usual, but in the long term, your diet will be directly reflected by your health.

Eating a healthy, balanced diet not only makes you feel good, it also helps you maintain the right weight for your height and reduces your risk of heart disease and many other ailments. It's now also thought that diet is linked to a third of all cancers. But it's important to remember that no matter how healthy someone's diet may be, there can never be an absolute guarantee they will not get some form of cancer or heart disease.

The easiest way to have a healthy diet is to ensure it's varied. It may help to imagine a large plate with all the food you eat in a day arranged on it. About a third should be filled with complex carbohydrates (bread, potatoes, rice, and pasta). Another third should be filled with a good variety of fruit and vegetables – fresh, frozen or canned, at least five servings a day. Just under a sixth of the plate should be filled with meat, fish, poultry, nuts or pulses. The same amount should be taken up by dairy foods, such as cheese, milk and yogurt (try to choose lower fat alternatives when you can). This leaves a thin portion for fatty and sugary foods like cakes, chips, soft drinks, and oils. Of course you may not have all these foods during the day.

Some foods are thought to be more protective than others, especially for certain cancers. Foods which contain antioxidants are beta carotene (the plant form of Vitamin A), Vitamin C and Vitamin E (see the Vitamins and minerals chart on pages 8–9 for the best sources.) Using the nutritional information on food and drink labels will also help you achieve a healthy diet. Simply adding up the amount of fat you eat each day will help you keep the balance right – but try to keep an eye on the sodium and sugar too. Check your intake against these guideline daily amounts, which are for men and women of average weight and physical activity:

Each Day	Men	Women
Fat	95g	70g
Calories	2,500	2,000
Sugars	70g	50g
Sodium	$2\frac{1}{2}$g	2g

Water, Drinks and Alcohol

Water is essential for life. Adults need 2–3 litres of water a day. However, some ways of drinking it are healthier than others.

Soft drinks can contain a lot of sugar and should be drunk sparingly. You shouldn't drink excessive amounts of coffee or tea either as they both contain the stimulant caffeine, which can lead to insomnia and headaches. Like most things, alcohol is fine as long as you don't overdo it. A couple of glasses of wine with a meal may actually help to reduce the risk of heart disease, but much more than three or four glasses has the reverse effect. A man can have three to four units a day and a woman can have two to three, but not every day and it does depend on your size. A unit is one glass of wine, a half pint of medium strength lager or beer or one measure of spirits. If you do have too much to drink, try to steer clear of alcohol for the next couple of days to give your body chance to recover.

Fertility and Pregnancy

Research shows that the chances of having a healthy pregnancy are significantly increased by eating healthily for at least three months before the baby is even conceived. Women should also take folic acid supplements until 12 weeks into their pregnancy, which greatly reduce the chances of the baby being born with spina bifida. Both men and women should limit their alcohol consumption – excessive amounts are linked to lower fertility and birth defects.

There is no need to eat much more than normal during pregnancy – an intake of about 2,400 calories should be adequate. Some additional nutrients are needed though: zinc for the baby's growth and sexual development and iron to treat or prevent anaemia. An extra serving of bread, cereal, pasta or some other complex carbohydrate is advised, together with the equivalent of a pint of milk to meet extra calcium and protein requirements.

Foods to avoid include liver, as it is very high in vitamin A and too much of it can harm the baby. Blue or soft cheeses, such as Camembert and Brie, and other unpasteurised foods such as patés should also be avoided, as there is a small risk of them being infected by a bacterium called listeria. Eggs, meat, fish and any ready-prepared meals should all be cooked thoroughly to avoid of other forms of food poisoning. Alcohol should be limited to the occasional glass of wine, but try to avoid it altogether during the first 12 weeks of pregnancy.

Children

Rapid growth means children need proportionately more nutrients than adults. However, because their stomachs are smaller than adults', they need smaller and more regular meals. Young children should not be given low-fat foods, such as skimmed milk – they need the extra calories of the full-fat versions. They can have low-fat foods once they're five years old and eating a varied diet.

Developing good eating habits in children early will mean they are more likely to eat healthily as they grow up. Try to get children used to the natural flavours of fresh fruit and vegetables, but don't force them to eat foods they don't like. Teeth are at greatest risk of decay during childhood, so avoid giving them too many sugary foods and drinks.

Being the Right Weight

If you're overweight, you're certainly not alone – more than a third of Australian people have the same problem. However, the seriously overweight run a higher risk of high blood pressure, heart disease and cancer, than people of normal weight. Following a healthy balanced diet within specific calorie guidelines is the best way to lose weight permanently. Women should aim for between 1,900–2,500 calories a day, depending on how active they are, while men need 2,500–3,000 calories. For a sensible weight loss of around 900g a week, aim for a reduction of 400 calories per day. Eat plenty of fruit, vegetables, and complex carbohydrates and cut down on things which are full of empty calories, like sweets, soft drinks, and alcohol. Avoid fatty foods and grill rather than fry things whenever you can.

Crash-dieting seldom works and all too often its results are short-lived. Fad diets are often dangerous, as they don't provide your body with the full range of nutrients it needs to function properly. The best way to reach or maintain a healthy weight is diet combined with exercise. Introduce exercise gradually and take advice from a doctor if you haven't exercised for a long time. If you do succumb to the odd treat, don't let it upset your long-term goal.

Being a Healthy Vegetarian

If you eat a good variety of dairy products, grains, vegetables, cereals and pulses, your diet will supply all the protein you need and be lower in saturated fat and include more fibre than the typical meat eater's. However, meat is the richest source of several key nutrients and vegetarians and vegans should take extra care to ensure they're getting enough iron, Vitamin B12, calcium and folate. Beans, lentils, dark leafy vegetables and wholegrain cereals provide iron; fortified breakfast cereals and dairy products are good sources of Vitamin B12; soya products, milk, cheese, yogurt and dark leafy vegetables supply calcium and most green leafy vegetables, peanuts, fortified breakfast cereals, and yeast extract are rich in folate. Iron deficiency is a common problem among women, especially vegans and vegetarians, in which case supplements may be necessary.

What Minerals and Vitamins Do

Our bodies can manufacture some vitamins and minerals on their own, but others must be obtained from our diet. We all have individual requirements and these change at different stages of our lives. The chart below outlines the best sources of the most important vitamins and minerals and briefly explains why our bodies need them.

Minerals

Some minerals, like calcium, are present in our bodies in quite large quantities, while others, like iron and zinc, are needed only in tiny amounts. Minerals help vitamins do their work, but they also carry out many functions of their own, like strengthening bones and teeth and maintaining a healthy immune system.

Vitamins

Every vitamin plays a specific part in helping our bodies function properly. For most of us, a well balanced diet provides all the vitamins we need, making supplements unnecessary. However, expectant mothers, young children, vegans and some vegetarians, the elderly and people with certain illnesses may benefit from taking supplements. But it can be dangerous to take large amounts of a supplement randomly. If you're in any doubt, ask your doctor or pharmacist for advice.

Vitamins are either water soluble or fat soluble. Vitamins B and C are water soluble and the body needs to replace them daily, as they cannot be stored. Vitamins A, D, and E are fat soluble and can be stored in the liver for about a week.

Minerals	Useful Sources	Major Roles
Calcium	Milk, cheese, yoghurt and other dairy products, canned sardines (eaten with their bones) white bread, green leafy vegetables and sesame seeds.	Needed for building bones and teeth and keeping them strong. Also vital for muscles, the nervous system, and blood clotting.
Iron	Offal (liver should not be eaten during pregnancy), lean meat, eggs, fortified breakfast cereals and bread, pulses, dried fruit and green leafy vegetables.	Essential for the production of red blood cells, which carry oxygen around the body.
Potassium	Milk, fruits (especially bananas), vegetables, meat, pulses, nuts, seeds, wholegrain cereals and potatoes.	Needed to maintain the fluid balance in the body and to keep heart rate and blood pressure normal.
Sodium	Occurs naturally in most foods. High levels in table salt, processed meats and many other processed foods.	Needed to maintain the fluid balance in the body. Essential for nerves and muscles to work properly.
Zinc	Meat, oysters, peanuts, milk, cheese, yoghurt and wholegrain cereals.	Essential for normal growth, wound healing and reproduction. Also needed for a healthy immune system.

Vitamins	Useful Sources	Major Roles
A (retinol in animal foods, or beta carotene in plant foods)	Liver (should not be eaten during pregnancy), oil-rich fish, full-fat milk, butter, cheese, green leafy vegetables and brightly coloured vegetables such as red capsicums.	Needed for bone growth, skin repair and good vision. Also acts as an antioxidant and helps the immune system.
B_1 (thiamin)	Meat, wholegrain cereals, fortified white bread, and breakfast cereals, nuts, pulses and potatoes.	Needed for energy production.
B_2 (riboflavin)	Milk, cheese, eggs, meat, fish, fortified breakfast cereals and yeast extract.	Needed to release the energy from food and for Vitamin B6 and niacin to work properly.
Niacin (nicotinic acid)	Lean meat, poultry, potatoes, bread, fortified breakfast cereals, wheatgerm and peanuts.	Helps maintain healthy skin and an efficient digestive system. Also needed to release energy.
B6 (pyridoxine)	Lean meat and poultry, fish, eggs, wholemeal bread, breakfast cereals, bananas and nuts.	Needed to make red blood cells, for a healthy immune system and to release energy from protein.
B12 (cyanocobalamin)	Lean meat, fish, shellfish, milk, eggs and some fortified breakfast cereals.	Essential for the growth and division of cells. Also helps prevent some forms of anaemia.
Folate (folic acid)	Bread, lightly-cooked green leafy vegetables, nuts, citrus fruit, bananas, potatoes, pulses and fortified breakfast cereals.	Needed for making protein and for passing on genetic information. It's crucial to have plenty of folate before conception and during the first stages of pregnancy.
C (ascorbic acid)	Blackcurrants, citrus fruit and juice, tomatoes, red, yellow and green capsicums, strawberries, potatoes and most green vegetables.	Needed for healthy cartilage, bones, skin, gums and teeth and the healing process. Also helps the body to absorb iron and is an important antioxidant.
D (calciferol)	Mostly comes from exposure to the sun. Also in fortified margarines and cereals, eggs and oil-rich fish such as tuna, salmon, and sardines.	Helps the body absorb the phosphorus and calcium it needs for healthy bones and teeth.
E (tocopherol)	Eggs, nuts, seeds, vegetable oils, sunflower margarines, wholemeal bread and fortified cereal products.	Good for skin and essential for skin repair. Also an antioxidant.

Soups, Salads and Starters

Dive headlong into these pages and you'll discover a wonderful array of recipes for the perfect light meal or appetiser. Whether it's a salad spruced up with duck and mango or a soup boldly blended with watercress, you'll be delighted at how tasty healthy eating can be. Not only is the result more satisfying, so is the process to achieve it. We've simplified each recipe so the experience is thoroughly enjoyable to ensure you return to these recipes time and time again. Happy hunting!

Plum Tomato, Lentil and Basil Soup

Preparation 30 mins **Cooking** 1 hr **Calories** 166 **Fat** 6g

6 tbsp continental lentils
1 kg plum tomatoes
1 tbsp olive oil
2 onions, chopped
2 tbsp sun-dried tomato purée
3 cups vegetable stock
1 bay leaf
black pepper
3 tbsp chopped fresh basil, plus extra leaves to garnish

1 Rinse the lentils, drain, then add them to a large saucepan of boiling water. Simmer, covered, for 25 minutes or until tender. Drain, rinse and set aside.

2 Meanwhile, place the tomatoes in a bowl, cover with boiling water, leave for 30 seconds, then drain. Remove the skins, deseed and chop. Heat the oil in a large saucepan, add the onions and cook for 10 minutes or until softened, stirring occasionally. Stir in the tomatoes, tomato purée, stock, bay leaf, and pepper. Bring to the boil and simmer, covered, stirring occasionally, for 25 minutes or until all the vegetables are cooked.

3 Remove the pan from the heat and cool for a few minutes. Remove and discard the bay leaf, then purée the soup until smooth in a food processor, liquidiser, or with a hand blender. Return to a clean pan, stir in the lentils and chopped basil, then reheat gently. Serve garnished with the fresh basil.

Serves 4

Watercress Soup

Preparation 35 mins **Cooking** 30 mins **Calories** 143 **Fat** 1g

1 tbsp sunflower oil
4 spring onions, finely chopped
1 leek, thinly sliced
250g potatoes, diced
1 cup watercress, chopped
2 cups vegetable stock
2 cups low-fat milk
black pepper, coarsely ground

1 Heat the oil in a large saucepan, then add the spring onions and leek and cook gently for 5 minutes or until softened, stirring occasionally. Add the potatoes and watercress to the spring onion mixture and cook for a further 3 minutes or until the watercress wilts, stirring occasionally.

2 Stir in the stock, milk and pepper. Bring to a boil, then reduce the heat and simmer, covered, for 20 minutes or until the potatoes are cooked and tender, stirring occasionally.

3 Remove the pan from the heat and cool for a few minutes. Purée the soup until smooth in a food processor, liquidiser, or with a hand blender. Return to a clean pan and reheat gently, until piping hot. Serve seasoned with the black pepper.

Serves 4

Note: This quick soup is full of goodness but it looks and tastes sophisticated enough to serve at any dinner party. For a change, use chopped spinach instead of watercress.

Cumin-Spiced Carrot Soup

Preparation 15 mins **Cooking** 40 mins **Calories** 116 **Fat** 4g

1 tbsp olive oil
1 large onion, chopped
1 clove garlic, crushed
3 sticks celery, chopped
1 tbsp ground cumin
680g carrots, thinly sliced
4 cups vegetable stock
black pepper
fresh coriander to garnish

1 Heat the oil in a large saucepan. Add the onion, garlic, and celery and fry gently for 5 minutes or until softened, stirring occasionally. Add the cumin and fry, stirring, for 1 minute to release its flavour.

2 Add the carrots, stock and pepper to the onion mixture and stir to combine. Bring to the boil and simmer, covered, for 30–35 minutes, until the vegetables are tender, stirring occasionally.

3 Remove the pan from the heat and cool for a few minutes. Purée the soup until smooth in a food processor, liquidiser, or with a hand blender. Return to a clean pan and reheat gently. Serve garnished with the fresh coriander.

Serves 4

Note: This thick soup, will really warm you up on a cold winter's night. To get the best flavour, spend a bit extra on fresh stock. Serve with naan bread.

Melon and Grapefruit Salad

Preparation 20 mins 1 hr chilling **Cooking** none **Calories** 57 **Fat** 1g

1 medium or 2 small melons, such as galia, charentais, honeydew, rockmelon or ogen

2 pink grapefruit

8 tbsp unsweetened fresh orange juice

1 tbsp orange liqueur, such as Cointreau or medium sherry (optional)

fresh mint to garnish

1. Cut the melon into segments and remove the seeds. Dice the flesh, or scoop it out using a melon baller. Place in a serving bowl.

2. Slice the top and bottom off each grapefruit and place on a work surface. Using a small serrated knife, cut off the skin and pith, following the curve of the fruit. Holding the grapefruit over a bowl, cut between the membranes to release the segments. Add the segments and juice to the melon.

3. Pour the orange juice and alcohol (if using) over the fruit and stir gently to mix. Cover and refrigerate for at least 1 hour before serving. Garnish with the fresh mint.

Serves 4

Note: If you want a light and refreshing starter, this is it. A dash of liqueur brings out the sweetness of the fruit. If you feel like it, add a few slices of parma ham.

Chicken Waldorf Salad

Preparation 15 mins 1 hr chilling **Cooking** none **Calories** 280 **Fat** 19g

250g cooked boneless chicken breasts, skinned and diced
4 sticks celery, thinly sliced
1 cup walnuts, roughly chopped
1 green and red-skinned eating apple
juice of $^1/_2$ lemon
250g mixed salad leaves
snipped fresh chives to garnish

Dressing

4 tbsp reduced-calorie mayonnaise
4 tbsp low-fat plain yoghurt
$^1/_2$ tsp finely grated lemon zest
freshly ground black pepper

1 Place the chicken in a bowl, add the celery and walnuts and stir to mix. Core, then dice the apples and toss them in the lemon juice to stop them browning. Add to the chicken and mix well.

2 To make the dressing, mix together the mayonnaise, yoghurt, lemon zest, and pepper in a small bowl. Then spoon the dressing over the chicken mixture and toss lightly to mix. Cover and refrigerate for at least 1 hour before serving.

3 To serve, arrange the salad leaves on serving plates and spoon the chicken mixture over. Garnish with the fresh chives.

Serves 4

Note: With its fresh lemony dressing, this simple Waldorf salad makes a great starter. To turn it into a deliciously light main course just serve it with some warm crusty bread.

Warm Duck and Mango Salad

Preparation 15 mins **Cooking** 5 mins **Calories** 233 **Fat** 13g

1 ripe mango
250g mixed dark salad leaves, such as baby spinach, lollo rosso, and rocket
1 cup sugar snap peas, chopped
4 spring onions, sliced diagonally
2 tsp sesame oil
250g boneless duck breast, skinned and cut into strips
fresh coriander to garnish

Dressing

3 tbsp extra virgin olive oil
juice of $\frac{1}{2}$ lime
1 tsp clear honey
2 tbsp chopped fresh coriander
freshly ground black pepper

Salad

1 Slice off the 2 fat sides of the mango close to the stone. Cut a criss-cross pattern across the flesh (but not the skin) of each side with a sharp knife. Push the skin inside out to expose the flesh and cut the cubes off. Place in a salad bowl with the salad leaves, peas, and spring onions, then toss together gently to mix.

Dressing

1 Whisk together the olive oil, lime juice, honey, coriander and pepper in a small bowl until thoroughly mixed.

2 Heat the sesame oil in a wok or large frying pan, add the duck and stir-fry over a high heat for 4–5 minutes until tender. Add the warm duck to the mango salad, drizzle over the dressing, then toss together to mix. Garnish with the fresh coriander.

Serves 4

Flaked Tuna Pasta Salad in Tomato Dressing

Preparation 15 mins **Cooking** 5 mins **Calories** 330 **Fat** 15g

2 cups whole wheat pasta
twists or shapes

4 spring onions, sliced, plus thin strips
to garnish

1 yellow capsicum, deseeded and
diced

1 cup sugar snap peas, chopped

1 cup canned corn, drained

1 cup canned tuna in water, drained
and flaked

Dressing

5 tbsp tomato paste

1 tbsp extra virgin olive oil

2 tsp balsamic vinegar

pinch of caster sugar

2 tbsp chopped fresh basil

freshly ground black pepper

1 Cook the pasta according to the instructions on the packet, until tender but firm to the bite. Drain, rinse under cold running water to cool, then drain thoroughly. Place in a serving bowl.

2 To make the dressing, whisk together the tomato paste, olive oil, vinegar, sugar, basil and black pepper in a bowl until thoroughly mixed. Pour the dressing over the pasta, then toss to mix well.

3 Add the sliced spring onions, capsicum, peas, corn and tuna to the pasta and toss lightly. Garnish with the spring onion strips.

Serves 4

Note: Pasta, colourful crunchy vegetables and flaked tuna are all bound together in a tangy tomato dressing. Use ridged or twisted pasta shapes as they hold the dressing well.

Marinated Mushrooms on a Bed of Leaves

Preparation 15 mins + 2 hrs marinating **Cooking** none **Calories** 181 **Fat** 6g

4 cups mixed mushrooms, such as shiitake, large open, button and oyster, thickly sliced

250g baby spinach leaves

30g watercress, thick stems discarded

fresh thyme to garnish

Dressing

3 tbsp extra virgin olive oil

2 tbsp unsweetened apple juice

2 tsp tarragon white wine vinegar

2 tsp Dijon mustard

1 clove garlic, crushed

1 tbsp mixed chopped fresh herbs, such as oregano, thyme, chives, basil and parsley

freshly ground black pepper

Dressing

1 Place the oil, apple juice, vinegar, mustard, garlic, herbs and pepper in a bowl and whisk with a fork to mix thoroughly.

Mushrooms

1 Pour the dressing over the mushrooms and stir well. Cover and place in the fridge for 2 hours.

2 Arrange the spinach and watercress on serving plates. Spoon the mushrooms and a little of the dressing over the top and toss lightly to mix. Garnish with the fresh thyme.

Serves 4

Note: Leave the mushrooms to absorb the flavours of the tangy mustard dressing, then pile them onto the spinach and watercress. Warm ciabatta goes well with this salad.

Curried Lentil Soup

Preparation 15 mins **Cooking** 65 mins **Calories** 49 **Fat** 3g

2 tbsp vegetable oil
1 onion, chopped
2 tsp curry powder
$\frac{1}{2}$ tsp ground cumin
1 tbsp tomato paste
1$\frac{1}{2}$ litres vegetable stock
125g red or green lentils
1 small head broccoli,
broken into florets
2 carrots, chopped
1 parsnip, chopped
1 stalk celery, chopped
freshly ground black pepper
1 tbsp chopped fresh parsley

1 Heat oil in a large saucepan, add onion, curry powder and cumin and cook, stirring occasionally, for 4–5 minutes or until onion is soft. Stir in tomato paste and stock and bring to the boil. Reduce heat, add lentils, cover and simmer for 30 minutes.

2 Add broccoli, carrots, parsnip and celery and cook, covered, for 30 minutes longer or until vegetables are tender. Season to taste with black pepper. Just prior to serving, stir in parsley.

Serves 6

Note: This thick and hearty soup can be made ahead of time and makes a great main meal.

Hummus with Vegetable Crudités

Preparation 15 mins **Cooking** none **Calories** 233 **Fat** 15g

2 cups canned chickpeas, drained and rinsed
juice of 1 lemon
3 tbsp extra virgin olive oil
2 tbsp light tahini
1 clove garlic, crushed
1/2 tsp ground coriander
1/2 tsp ground cumin
freshly ground black pepper
500g mixed vegetables, such as capsicum, carrots, zucchini, cauliflower, broccoli, mushrooms, radishes, baby asparagus and spring onions

1   Blend the chickpeas, lemon juice, olive oil, tahini, garlic, coriander, cumin and black pepper in a food processor, or with a hand blender, until they form a coarse hummus paste.

2   Slice the capsicum, carrots and zucchini into sticks and cut the cauliflower and broccoli into florets. Wipe the mushrooms and trim the radishes, asparagus and spring onions. Arrange the vegetables on a serving plate. Spoon the hummus into a serving bowl and serve with the crudités.

Serves 4

Note: Vary the quantities of coriander and cumin to make this Middle Eastern dip as spicy as you like. You can also change the amounts of garlic and lemon to suit your taste.

Grilled Vegetable Bruschetta

Preparation 15 mins **Cooking** 5 mins **Calories** 275 **Fat** 11g

1 red or yellow capsicum, deseeded and sliced into strips
1 zucchini, halved and thinly sliced lengthways
1 red onion, thinly sliced
2 large plum tomatoes, thickly sliced
3 tbsp extra virgin olive oil
2 tsp wholegrain mustard
freshly ground black pepper
1 ciabatta loaf, cut into 8 slices, or 8 slices from a baguette
1 clove garlic, halved
8 black olives, pitted and thinly sliced
fresh basil to garnish

1. Preheat the grill to high and line the grill rack with foil. Place the capsicum, zucchini, onion and tomatoes in a bowl. Whisk together $\frac{2}{3}$ of oil, the mustard and the black pepper, then pour over the vegetables and toss gently to coat.

2. Spread the vegetables in a single layer on the grill rack and grill for 3–4 minutes on each side, until lightly browned. Set aside and keep warm.

3. Toast the bread slices on both sides under the grill and, while still hot, rub the garlic halves over one side of each piece of toast. Divide the vegetables between the toast slices, piling them onto the garlicky sides. Scatter over the olives and drizzle over the remaining oil. Garnish with the fresh basil and serve.

Serves 4–6

Note: This Mediterranean snack is great for drinks parties. Rubbing garlic over the toast gives it a sweet taste that sets off the flavour of the grilled vegetables.

Belgium Endive Snack Ring

Preparation 15 mins **Cooking** 35 mins **Calories** 80 **Fat** 5g

4 large endive heads
$\frac{1}{4}$ cup margarine
$\frac{1}{4}$ cup plain flour
sprinkling grated nutmeg
3 eggs

1. Trim endive and blanch in boiling salted water for 5 minutes. Plunge pan into cold water quickly.

2. Drain well and chop endive into small pieces. Preheat oven to 180°C

3. Melt margarine in a saucepan, stir in flour and cook for one minute. Gradually stir in milk and bring to boil, stirring continuously and allow to simmer until thickened.

4. Season with salt, pepper and nutmeg.

5. Remove pan from heat and stir in chopped endive. Allow to cool slightly,then beat in the eggs.

6. Turn into greased ring mould and bake for 30 minutes.

7. Un-mould onto a warmed serving dish and serve hot.

Serves 4

Note: Best as a hot snack, but can be served as an entree or as an accompaniment to the main meal.

Meat Dishes

Many health-conscious cooks avoid meat in their pursuit of healthy living, yet properly prepared it can be a delicious and nutritious addition to any diet. Meat has multiple uses, from kebabs and casseroles to curries and burgers, so you can banish the bland steak-and-veggies meal forever. Our serving suggestions will show you how to make ordinary ingredients deliver results that are nothing less than extraordinary. Find out how red wine can create a scrumptious meat pie, and how apricot can add a sweet twist to a lamb casserole for a new family favourite. Go 'round the block' once with our recipes and you're sure to become best friends with your butcher.

Lamb and Capsicum Kebabs with Chilli Sauce

Preparation 20 mins + 2 hrs marinating **Cooking** 40 mins **Calories** 249 **Fat** 11g

$^1/_2$ cup red wine

1 tbsp olive oil

juice of $^1/_2$ lemon

1 tbsp chopped fresh rosemary

freshly ground black pepper

350g lean boneless leg of lamb, cut into 12 cubes

1 red and 1 yellow capsicum, each deseeded and cut into 8 pieces

16 button mushrooms

4 metal skewers

Sauce

2 cups canned chopped tomatoes

$^1/_2$ cup vegetable stock

1 small onion, finely chopped

1 green chilli, deseeded and finely chopped

1 tbsp tomato paste

1 clove garlic, crushed

freshly ground black pepper

Kebabs

1   In a non-metallic bowl, mix 4 tablespoons of the red wine and the oil, lemon juice, rosemary and black pepper. Add the lamb, turn to coat, then cover and place in the fridge for 2 hours.

2   Preheat the grill to high. Thread the lamb, capsicums and mushrooms onto 4 metal skewers, dividing evenly. Reserve the marinade.

3   Meanwhile, grill the kebabs for 12–18 minutes until the lamb is tender, turning occasionally and basting with the marinade. Serve with the chilli sauce.

Sauce

1   Place the tomatoes, stock, onion, chilli, tomato paste, garlic, black pepper and remaining wine in a saucepan and stir. Bring to a boil, then reduce the heat and simmer, uncovered, for 15–20 minutes, until the sauce has thickened, stirring occasionally.

Serves 4

Note: The rosemary in the marinade goes beautifully with large succulent chunks of lamb, while a hot chilli sauce adds some bite. If you prefer, use apple juice instead of wine.

Lamb and Apricot Casserole

Preparation 15 mins **Cooking** 2 hrs **Calories** 374 **Fat** 14g

1 tbsp sunflower oil
500g lean boneless lamb leg or fillet, cut into 2cm cubes
1 large onion, chopped
1 clove garlic, finely chopped
2 tbsp plain flour
1 tsp ground coriander
1 tsp ground cumin
1 $\frac{1}{2}$ cups vegetable stock
$\frac{2}{3}$ cup red wine
1 cup baby button mushrooms
1 tbsp tomato paste
1 bouquet garni
freshly ground black pepper
1 cup dried apricots
2 tbsp chopped fresh coriander, plus extra leaves to garnish

1   Preheat the oven. Heat the oil in a flameproof and ovenproof casserole dish on the stove. Add the lamb and cook for about 5 minutes or until browned. Remove and keep warm.

2   Add the onion and garlic to the juices in the dish and cook for 5 minutes, or until softened. Return the lamb to the dish with the flour, coriander, and cumin, and cook for 1 minute, stirring. Slowly add the stock and wine and bring to the boil, stirring. Stir in the mushrooms, tomato paste, bouquet garni, and pepper. Cover and cook in the oven for 1 hour.

3   Stir in the apricots and cook for a further 30 minutes or until the lamb is tender. Remove and discard the bouquet garni, stir in the chopped coriander, then garnish with more fresh coriander.

Serves 4

Oven temperature   160°C, 325°F, Gas 3

Note: Dried apricots give a sweetness to this delicious casserole, but dried pears or peaches also work well. Serve it with some steamed broccoli and bread, rice or jacket potatoes.

Braised Pork with Apples

Preparation 15 mins **Cooking** 2 hrs **Calories** 242 **Fat** 11g

1 tbsp sunflower oil

4 boneless lean pork loin steaks or medallions

4 spring onions, thinly sliced

1 cup mushrooms, sliced

1 tbsp plain flour

1 cup vegetable stock

$\frac{1}{2}$ cup dry cider

2 tsp Dijon or wholegrain mustard

freshly ground black pepper

2 large eating apples, peeled, cored and sliced

fresh flat-leaf parsley to garnish

1 Preheat the oven. Heat the oil in a non-stick frying pan. Add the pork and cook for 5 minutes or until browned, turning once, then transfer to a casserole dish.

2 Add the spring onions and mushrooms to the frying pan and cook gently for 5 minutes or until softened. Add the flour and cook for 1 minute, stirring. Slowly add the stock and cider, stirring until smooth, then add the mustard and pepper. Bring to the boil and continue stirring for 2–3 minutes, until thickened.

3 Place the apple slices on top of the pork steaks and pour over the sauce. Cover and cook in the oven for 1–1 $\frac{1}{2}$ hours, until the pork is tender and cooked through. Garnish with the parsley.

Serves 4

Note: Pork goes beautifully with the slight tartness of cooked apples. In this succulent slow-cooked casserole, the cider brings out the taste of the apples even more.

Oven temperature 160°C, 325°F, Gas 3

Peppered Beef Steaks with Red Onion Salsa

Preparation 15 mins + 1hr standing **Cooking** 5 mins **Calories** 247 **Fat** 12g

2 tbsp mixed peppercorns
4 lean sirloin, rump or fillet steaks, trimmed of fat
fresh parsley to garnish

Salsa

3 tomatoes
2 tbsp tomato juice
2 tbsp olive oil
1 red onion, finely chopped
2 tsp horseradish sauce
1 tbsp chopped fresh parsley
freshly ground black pepper

Salsa

1 Place the tomatoes in a bowl, cover with boiling water and leave for 30 seconds. Drain, peel off the skins, deseed and finely chop. Put the flesh into a bowl with the tomato juice, ½ the oil, the red onion, horseradish sauce, parsley and black pepper, and mix together well. Cover and set aside for 1 hour.

Steak

1 Preheat the grill to medium. Crush the peppercorns with a pestle and mortar, or rolling pin. Brush the steaks all over with the rest of the oil, then coat with the crushed peppercorns.

2 Place the steaks on the grill rack and grill for 4–5 minutes each side, until browned and cooked to your liking. Serve with the red onion salsa and garnish with the fresh parsley.

Serves 4

Spiced Beef and Carrot Burgers

Preparation 15 mins **Cooking** 15 mins **Calories** 231 **Fat** 8g

500g extra lean minced beef
2 carrots, coarsely grated
1 cup mushrooms, finely chopped
1 large onion or 3 spring onions,
finely chopped
1 cup fresh whole-wheat breadcrumbs
2 tbsp tomato purée
1 medium egg, lightly beaten
1 clove garlic, crushed
2 tsp ground cumin
2 tsp ground coriander
1 tsp hot chilli powder
freshly ground black pepper

1 Preheat the grill to medium. Place all the ingredients in a large bowl and mix together well.

2 Shape the mixture into 4 round, flat burgers, using your hands. Grill for about 10–15 minutes, until the burgers are lightly browned and cooked to your liking, turning once.

Serves 4

Note: These healthy burgers will be popular with all the family. Try serving them in wholemeal buns piled high with crisp salad leaves, slices of tomato, and tangy relish.

Sweet Lamb Chop Curry

Preparation 25 mins **Cooking** 70 mins **Calories** 292 **Fat** 4g

6 forequarter lamb chops
1 tbsp olive oil
1 large onion, finely chopped
1 clove garlic, crushed
1 1/2 tbsp Madras-style curry powder
1/2 tsp ground ginger
2 cups water
salt and pepper
3/4 cup mixed dried fruit
1 tsp brown sugar
1/2 cinnamon stick
1/2 cup plain yoghurt (optional)

1 Trim any excess fat from the chops. Wipe over with kitchen paper. Heat the oil in a large, heavy-based saucepan or lidded skillet. Add the onion and garlic and fry until golden over moderate heat. Remove the onion with a slotted spoon and set aside. Increase the heat and brown chops quickly on both sides. Do only 2–3 at a time. Remove to a plate and drain almost all fat from the pan.

2 Add the curry powder and ginger to the hot saucepan and stir over heat to roast until aroma rises. Stir in the water, lifting the pan juices as you stir. Season with salt and pepper.

3 Return the lamb and onion to the pan, cover and simmer for 1 hour. Add the dried fruit, sugar and cinnamon stick, and simmer for approximately 1 hour, until the lamb is very soft and tender. Add more water during cooking if necessary. Remove the chops to a hot serving platter. Stir the yoghurt into the sauce (if using) and pour the sauce over the chops. Serve with boiled rice.

Serves 4–6

Meatballs with Tomato Relish

Preparation 25 mins **Cooking** 5 mins **Calories** 106 each **Fat** 2g each

250g brown onions, finely chopped
1 kg minced beef
$^1\!/_2$ cup breadcrumbs
2 eggs
1 tbsp mint, chopped
$^1\!/_4$ cup water
salt and freshly ground black pepper
2 cups vegetable oil, for frying
sprinkle of plain flour

Tomato Relish

1 kg Roma tomatoes, chopped
2 brown onions, chopped
1 cup sugar
$^1\!/_2$ cup brown vinegar
2 tbsp tomato paste
1 tsp salt
$^1\!/_2$ tbsp dry mustard
$^1\!/_4$ tsp cayenne pepper (optional)

Meatballs

1   In a bowl, combine the chopped onions, minced beef, breadcrumbs, eggs, mint, water, and salt and pepper. Squeeze the mixture between your fingers making sure it's well combined.

2   Using 2 tablespoons of mixture for each meatball, shape into balls, then toss in a little flour, and shake off the excess. Flatten each ball slightly into the palm of your hand.

3   Heat the oil in a pan and cook each meatball for approximately 3 minutes each side until they are dark brown and cooked through.

4   Drain on absorbent paper.

Tomato relish

1   Place all ingredients in a medium-sized saucepan and bring to a boil, then simmer for one hour (until mixture becomes thick and pulpy). Check the seasoning, and add salt and black pepper if desired.

2   Remove from the heat and store in a sterilised jar in the refrigerator for up to one week. With the remainder of the Tomato Relish, serve hot or cold with the meatballs.

Makes 40

Carbonada Griolla

Preparation 15 mins **Cooking** 55 mins **Calories** 410 **Fat** 2g

2 tbsp oil
1 clove garlic, crushed
1 large onion, chopped
1 kg boned shoulder of veal, cut into 2cm cubes
1 cup peeled, canned tomatoes
1 ½ cups beef stock
1 tsp chopped thyme
2 tbsp chopped parsley
salt and pepper
1 medium potato, cubed
1 sweet potato, cubed
250g pumpkin, cubed
2 fresh corn cobs, cut into thick slices
½ cup short grain rice
4 large dried peaches, halved
4 large dried pears, halved

1 Heat the oil in a large saucepan and sauté the garlic and onion. Add the veal, and quickly stir over a high heat to brown lightly.

2 Add the tomatoes, stock, thyme and parsley and season with salt and pepper. Bring to the boil, then turn down the heat and simmer for 25 minutes.

3 Add the cubed vegetables, corn, rice and dried fruits. Cover and simmer for 25 minutes. Stir occasionally during cooking and add extra stock if necessary. Adjust seasoning before serving.

Serves 6

Ham Steaks with Fruity Sauce

Preparation 50 mins **Cooking** 10 mins **Calories** 273 **Fat** 3g

Fruity Sauce

$1/2$ cup mixed dried fruit

$1 1/2$ cups water

$1/2$ tsp salt

2 tbsp brown sugar

1 tsp Worcestershire sauce

3–4 drops Tabasco sauce

1 tbsp cornflour blended with a little water

Ham Steaks

butter for frying

6 ham steaks

Ham steaks

1   Heat the butter in a frying pan and fry the ham steaks on both sides until rosy brown. Serve the with fruity sauce and vegetable accompaniments.

Fruity Sauce

1   To make the fruity sauce, place the mixed dried fruit in a saucepan, add the water and soak for $1/2$ hour. Add the remaining sauce ingredients (except the cornflour) and bring to a boil. Turn down and simmer, covered, for 20 minutes. Add the blended cornflour and stir until the sauce thickens.

Serves 3–4

Pork with Mango Couscous

Preparation 30 mins **Cooking** 1¾ hrs **Calories** 180 **Fat** 8g

2 kg boneless pork loin, rind removed and trimmed of all visible fat

Mango Couscous Stuffing

90g couscous
¹/₂ cup boiling water
¹/₂ mango, chopped
2 spring onions, chopped
3 tbsp chopped fresh coriander
2 tsp finely grated lime rind
¹/₂ tsp garam masala
1 egg white, lightly beaten
1 tbsp lime juice

Creamy Wine Sauce
¹/₂ cup chicken stock
¹/₂ cup white wine
2 tbsp low-fat natural yoghurt

1   To make stuffing, place couscous in a bowl, pour boiling water over and toss with a fork until couscous absorbs all the liquid. Add mango, spring onions, coriander, lime rind, garam masala, egg white and lime juice and mix to combine.

2   Lay pork out flat and spread stuffing evenly over surface. Roll up firmly and secure with string. Place pork on a wire rack set in a roasting tin, pour in 2¹/₂cm water and bake for 1¹/₂ hours or until pork is cooked to your liking. Place pork on a serving platter, set aside and keep warm.

3   To make sauce, skim excess fat from pan juices, stir in stock and wine and bring to the boil over a medium heat. Reduce heat and simmer for 10 minutes or until sauce reduces by half. Remove tin from heat and whisk in yoghurt. Slice pork and serve with sauce.

Serves 8

Note: On completion of cooking, remove meat from oven, cover and stand in a warm place for 10–15 minutes before carving. Standing allows the juices to settle and makes carving easier.

Individual Beef and Red Wine Pies

Preparation 30 mins **Cooking** 75 mins **Calories** 325 **Fat** 9g

2 tsp peanut oil

1 large onion, chopped

2 cloves garlic, crushed

1 kg beef chuck steak, trimmed of all fat and cubed

2 tbsp plain flour

2 tbsp reduced salt tomato paste

1 ½ cups red wine

1 ½ cups reduced salt beef stock

2 carrots, thinly sliced

2 cups Swiss brown mushrooms, quartered

2 tbsp fresh thyme, chopped

2 tbsp fresh parsley, chopped

2 sheets canola puff pastry, defrosted

6 sprigs thyme

1 tbsp low or reduced-fat milk

1. Preheat the oven. You will need six 2-cup capacity ovenproof pie dishes.

2. Heat the oil in a large pot, add the onion and cook over a medium heat for 5 minutes or until golden. Add the garlic and the beef and cook for 5 minutes until the beef is browned.

3. Add the flour and tomato paste and cook for a further 2 minutes, stirring constantly. Stir in the red wine and stock and bring to the boil. Add the carrots, mushrooms and chopped thyme. Reduce the heat, cover and simmer for about 1 hour, then remove the lid and cook for a further 45 minutes until the beef is tender and the sauce is reduced and thickened. Stir through the parsley, transfer to a bowl and allow the filling to cool completely.

4. Using the top of a pie dish as a guide, cut 6 circles from the pastry, about 2cm larger than the dish. Spoon the cooled filling into the ovenproof pie dishes. Brush the edges of each pastry circle with a little water, then cover the dishes (damp side down), pressing the pastry to the side of the dish to seal. Cut a small cross in the top of each pie, insert a sprig of thyme, and lightly brush with the milk.

5. Bake for 20–25 minutes, or until the pastry is crisp and golden and the filling is hot. Serve the pies with mashed potato and steamed beans.

Makes 6

Oven temperature 200°C, 400°F, Gas 6

Lamb Shanks with Broad Beans, Olives and Risoni

Preparation 20 mins **Cooking** 1 hr **Calories** 452 **Fat** 3g

2 tbsp olive oil
2 cloves garlic, crushed
4 lamb shanks
1 onion, chopped
2 cups beef stock
4 sprigs oregano
2 tbsp tomato paste
2 cups water
1 cup risoni (rice)
1 cup broad beans
$1/2$ cup olives
2 tsp fresh oregano, chopped
salt and freshly ground pepper

1 Heat the oil in a large saucepan, add the garlic, lamb shanks and onion and cook for 5 minutes or until the shanks are lightly browned.

2 Add the beef stock, oregano sprigs, tomato paste and $1/2$ the water. Bring to the boil, reduce the heat and leave to simmer with the lid on for 40 minutes.

3 Remove the shanks, slice the meat off the bone and set aside.

4 Add the risoni and the remaining water, cook for a further 5 minutes, then add the beans, olives, meat, oregano, salt and pepper, cook for 5 minutes more and serve.

Serves 4–6

Note: If broad beans are large, peel off outer skin.

Beef with Artichokes, Olives and Oregano

Preparation 30 mins **Cooking** 1 hr Calories 419 **Fat** 7g

2 tbsp olive oil
750g scotch fillet
1 clove garlic, crushed
1 bunch spring onions, trimmed and halved
1/2 cup white wine
1 cup beef stock
1 tbsp tomato paste
2 tsp oregano, chopped
salt and freshly ground pepper
2 globe artichokes, trimmed and quartered
1/3 cup olives, pitted

1 Preheat the oven.
2 In a large, heavy-based oven-proof dish, heat 1 tablespoon olive oil, add the meat and sear quickly on all sides. Remove and set aside.
3 Heat remaining olive oil, add the garlic and spring onions, and cook for 2–3 minutes. Add the white wine, cook for 1 minute, then add the beef stock, tomato paste, oregano and salt and pepper. Bring to the boil, return the meat to the dish, add the artichokes, cover and bake for 30–40 minutes.
4 Add the olives in the last 5 minutes of cooking time.
5 Slice the meat and arrange with the vegetables. Pour the sauce over meat and vegetables.

Serves 4

Note: Trim the artichokes of their outer leaves and stems and place them in a bowl of water with lemon juice to stop them going brown.

Oven temperature 180°C, 350°F, Gas 4

Poultry Dishes

Create a stir at the dinner table with a bold new blend of seasonings to pep up your poultry. You will discover fresh and exciting recipes that take chicken into a whole new dimension. Try your hand at lathering a chicken thigh in a fruity mint salsa, or splashing a chicken breast fillet with a citrus and yoghurt sauce. Our expert team has done the 'hard yards' to ensure these recipes taste just as delectable as they sound – yet can be easily incorporated into your daily cooking routine.

Chicken Rolls with Orange Currant Sauce

Preparation 30 mins **Cooking** 30 mins **Calories** 200 **Fat** 9g

2 tsp grated orange zest

4 strips thinly peeled orange zest, cut into thin strips (julienne)

juice of 3 oranges

1 small onion, finely chopped and fried in a little butter

¼ cup fresh breadcrumbs

2 tbsp currants

1 kg chicken thigh fillets

salt and pepper

2 ginger nut biscuits, finely crushed

2 tbsp brandy

1 Mix together the grated orange zest, 2 tablespoons of the orange juice, the fried onions and the breadcrumbs. Flatten chicken thigh fillets with a meat mallet, smooth side down, and sprinkle with salt and pepper. Place a teaspoon of filling onto each fillet, pressing on well. Roll up and secure with a toothpick.

2 Heat butter or oil in a heavy-based frying pan and brown on all sides. Reduce heat and add remaining orange juice, scraping up any browned juices with the back of a spoon. Add currants and a pinch of salt and pepper. Cover and simmer for 20 minutes, until chicken rolls are tender. Remove rolls to a warm serving platter and, keep hot.

3 To the pan juices add the crushed ginger nut biscuits. Stir over low heat until thickened. If a thinner consistency is desired, add extra orange juice or water. Pour over chicken rolls and garnish with blanched julienne orange zest.

Serves 6

Chicken in Strawberry Sauce

Preparation 15 mins **Cooking** 35 mins **Calories** 144 **Fat** 7g

400g chicken breast fillets
4 shallots, finely sliced
salt, pepper
1/2 cup hot water
1 tbsp strawberry jam
2 tbsp tarragon vinegar
1 tsp finely chopped mint
2 strawberries, sliced into strips
1 tsp cornflour
1 tsp water
2 strawberries for garnish

1 Place breast fillets and shallots in a covered pan, sprinkle with salt and pepper and add water. Bring to simmering point, turn down heat and simmer, covered, for 20 minutes until tender. Remove poached fillets to a plate and keep hot.

2 Reduce the liquid in the pan a little, stir in the strawberry jam, vinegar, mint and sliced strawberries. Simmer 1 minute. Blend cornflour with water, add to sauce and stir until it boils and thickens.

3 Place fillets on individual plates, spoon over sauce and garnish with fresh strawberry and mint sprig. Serve with steamed potatoes and snow peas or beans.

Serves 2

Note: If a richer coloured sauce is desired, add 1 drop of red food colour to the sauce.

Chicken Kebabs with Yoghurt and Lemon Sauce

Preparation 20 mins + marinating **Cooking** 10 mins **Calories** 283 **Fat** 3g

24 wooden satay skewers
1 cup plain yoghurt
2 cloves garlic, crushed
1$\frac{1}{2}$ tsp paprika, ground
1$\frac{1}{2}$ tsp cumin seeds
4 tbsp lemon juice
2 tbsp parsley, chopped
2 tsp oregano, chopped
freshly ground black pepper
oil for cooking
6 chicken thigh fillets, cubed

1. Soak the wooden satay skewers in cold water for 30 minutes.
2. Place the yoghurt, garlic, paprika, cumin seeds, lemon juice, parsley, oregano and pepper and mix until combined.
3. Place the chicken on the satay and brush over skewers with $\frac{1}{2}$ the mixture. Leave to marinate in refrigerator for 2–3 hours.
4. Heat the oil on the barbecue (or chargrill pan), add the chicken kebabs and cook 4–5 minutes each side.
5. Serve with the remaining marinade mixture.

Serves 4

Mushroom and Tarragon Stuffed Chicken

Preparation 30 mins **Cooking** 35 mins **Calories** 207 **Fat** 10g

2 tbsp olive oil
1 small leek, finely chopped
1 small zucchini, finely chopped
1 clove garlic, crushed
$1/2$ cup button mushrooms, finely chopped
$1/2$ cup oyster or shiitake mushrooms, finely chopped
1 tbsp chopped fresh tarragon, plus extra leaves to garnish
freshly ground black pepper
4 skinless boneless chicken breasts
cocktail sticks

1 Preheat the oven. Heat $1/2$ the oil in a saucepan. Add the leek, zucchini, garlic and mushrooms, and cook for 5 minutes, stirring, until softened. Remove from the heat and stir in the tarragon and pepper.

2 Place the chicken breasts between 2 large sheets of baking paper. Beat to an even thickness with a rolling pin. Spread the stuffing evenly over each breast. Roll up, folding in the ends and secure with wetted cocktail sticks. Brush with the remaining oil and place on a non-stick baking sheet.

3 Cook in the oven for 30–35 minutes, until the juices run clear when pierced with a skewer. Remove the cocktail sticks and cut each roll into 2cm slices, then garnish with fresh tarragon.

Serves 4

Note: The aniseed flavour of fresh tarragon combines beautifully with chicken and mushrooms. Try serving these neat slices with potatoes and some roasted cherry tomatoes.

Oven temperature 180°C, 350°F, Gas 4

Chicken and Broccoli Lasagna

Preparation 30 mins + 20 mins standing **Cooking** 45 mins **Calories** 600 **Fat** 6g

4 cups low-fat milk

2 spring onions, sliced

2 sticks celery, sliced

2 bay leaves

1 cup broccoli, cut into small florets

2 tbsp sunflower oil

1 onion, chopped

1 clove garlic, crushed

1 cup mushrooms, sliced

2 zucchini, sliced

3 tbsp sunflower spread

3 tbsp plain flour

$^1/_2$ cup low-fat aged Cheddar cheese, finely grated

1 $^1/_2$ cups cooked boneless chicken breasts, skinned and diced

freshly ground black pepper

170g egg lasagna verdi sheets

1 Put the milk, spring onions, celery and bay leaves into a small saucepan, and bring to the boil. Set aside to infuse for 20 minutes. Cook the broccoli florets in a saucepan of boiling water for 2 minutes. Drain and set aside. Heat the oil in a frying pan and cook the onion, garlic, mushrooms and zucchini for 5 minutes or until softened.

2 Preheat the oven. Put the sunflower spread and flour in a pan and strain in the milk, then bring to the boil, whisking. Simmer for 3 minutes, stirring. Set aside 1 $^1/_4$ cups of the sauce and stir $^1/_2$ cup of the Cheddar, the onion mixture and the broccoli, chicken and pepper into the remaining sauce.

3 Spoon $^1/_2$ the chicken mixture into a shallow ovenproof dish. Cover with $^1/_2$ the lasagna sheets. Repeat, then pour over the reserved sauce and sprinkle with the rest of the Cheddar. Cook for 45 minutes or until golden.

Serves 4

Oven temperature 180°C, 350°F, Gas 4

Turkey Steaks with Mustard Sauce

Preparation 10 mins **Cooking** 15 mins **Calories** 252 **Fat** 3g

1 tbsp olive oil

4 skinless boneless turkey breast steaks

Sauce

1 tbsp sunflower spread

1 tbsp plain flour

1 cups low-fat milk

1–2 tbsp wholegrain mustard

freshly ground black pepper

fresh herbs, such as basil, chives or coriander to garnish

1. Heat the oil in a non-stick frying pan. Add the turkey steaks and cook for 15 minutes, or until tender and lightly browned, turning once.

2. Meanwhile, melt the sunflower spread in a saucepan. Add the flour and gently cook for 1 minute, stirring. Remove from the heat and gradually add the milk, stirring until smooth.

3. Return to the heat and slowly bring to the boil, stirring continuously until the sauce thickens. Simmer for 2 minutes, stirring occasionally. Stir in the mustard and pepper.

4. Spoon the mustard sauce over the turkey steaks and serve garnished with the fresh herbs.

Serves 4

Festive Chicken Salad

Preparation 30 mins + 1 hr refrigeration **Cooking** 35 mins **Calories** 156 **Fat** 14g

1 1/2 kg chicken, roasted
1 bunch English spinach
1 coral lettuce
1 radicchio lettuce
6 slices of bread
2 tbsp olive oil
4 rashers bacon
1 can mango slices or 1 fresh mango, sliced
2 small Spanish onions, thinly sliced
2 avocados, peeled and sliced

Dressing
1/2 cup olive oil
1/4 cup vinegar
1 tsp Dijon mustard
1 tsp sugar
1 tsp fresh thyme
1 tsp lemon zest

Garnish
nasturtium flowers

Dressing

1 Combine all dressing ingredients together in a screw topped jar and shake well. Stand 30 minutes to concentrate flavour.

Salad

1 Wash the spinach and lettuce, drain well, place in a clean kitchen towel and refrigerate for 1 hour to crisp. Tear into bite sized pieces.

2 Remove crusts from bread, cut into small dice. Fry until golden and crisp in hot oil. Drain on paper towels.

3 Dice the bacon and fry until crisp.

4 Drain the mango slices, cut each in half lengthwise or peel and slice the fresh mango into strips.

5 Remove breast from chicken, discard skin and cut into strips. Remove leg and thigh portions, discard skin and slice thinly.

6 Toss together spinach, lettuce, onion slices, croutons and bacon. Toss well with 1/2 of the dressing. Spread onto a large tray or serving platter then arrange 1/2 of the chicken slices on top, leaving a border of salad. Place a row of avocado slices over the chicken, indenting to show some chicken, then more chicken slices followed by mango. Top with a small pile of chicken. Drizzle remaining dressing over the layers and garnish top with nasturtium flowers.

Serves 15

Cajun Chicken with Pawpaw Salsa

Preparation 15 mins **Cooking** 35 mins **Calories** 162 **Fat** 8g

4 boneless chicken breast fillets, skinned and trimmed of all visible fat

2 cloves garlic, crushed

1 tbsp onion salt

1 tbsp ground white pepper

1 tbsp cracked black pepper

2 tsp cayenne pepper

1 tbsp paprika

1 tbsp dried mixed herbs

Pawpaw Salsa

1 small pawpaw, diced

1 cucumber, diced

2 tbsp mint leaves

2 tbsp low-fat natural yoghurt

2 tbsp lime juice

1 Rub the chicken with crushed garlic. Place onion salt, white pepper, black pepper, cayenne pepper, paprika and mixed herbs in a bowl and mix to combine.

2 Rub spice mixture over the chicken, place on a non-stick baking tray and bake for 25–30 minutes or until chicken is tender. Cover and stand for 5 minutes before serving.

Pawpaw Salsa

3 Place pawpaw, cucumber, mint, yoghurt and lime juice in a bowl and mix to combine. Serve with the chicken.

Serves 4

Note: After rubbing spice mixture onto the chicken, wash your hands and do not touch your face or lips as the cayenne pepper causes burning.

Oven temperature 180°C, 350°F, Gas 4

Grilled Tenderloins with Spiced Pumpkin

Preparation 40 mins **Cooking** 2 mins **Calories** 261 **Fat** 1g

500g chicken tenderloins
2 tbsp lemon juice
1 clove garlic, crushed
2 tsp olive oil
250g potatoes, peeled, cut and rinsed
1 kg pumpkin, cut and peeled
2 tbsp fat-reduced milk
1 tsp nutmeg
1 tbsp chopped coriander or parsley
canola oil spray
1 medium onion, thinly sliced
2 medium tomatoes, sliced

1 Place the tenderloins in a non-metal dish. Add the lemon juice, garlic and oil. Cover and marinate for 40 minutes in the refrigerator.

2 Meanwhile, boil the potatoes and pumpkin until tender, drain, and mash. Add the milk, nutmeg and coriander or parsley. Set aside and keep hot. Heat preferred grill to high, spray lightly with canola oil spray and place on the tenderloins, onion, and tomatoes. Cook the tenderloins for 2 minutes each, turn the tomatoes and onion and cook until soft.

3 Pile the spiced pumpkin onto 4 heated plates, arrange the grilled tenderloins over the pumpkin and top with grilled tomato and onion.

Serves 4

Steamed Dinner for One

Preparation 10 mins **Cooking** 20 mins **Calories** 121 **Fat** 8g

125g chicken stir-fry, cut into strips
3 small new potatoes, scrubbed
1 small carrot, cut into fine strips
a knob of butter
2 tsp lemon juice
lemon pepper
2 shallots, cut diagonally
1/2 stick celery, cut into fine strips

1 Place potatoes in a saucepan and cover with water, add salt. Bring to the boil.

2 Grease a dinner plate well with butter, place on the chicken strips, spreading to make 1 layer, and arrange carrot and celery strips on plate. Sprinkle chicken with the lemon juice and lemon pepper. Add an extra dot of butter if desired. Place plate over the saucepan containing the potatoes and cover with an overturned dinner plate. Allow to cook for 20 minutes until chicken is tender.

3 Remove potato from saucepan and serve with the steamed chicken and vegetables.

Serves 1–2

Orange Chicken

Preparation 10 mins + 2 hrs marinating **Cooking** 30 mins **Calories** 165 **Fat** 8g

4 boneless chicken breasts, skinned

2 tsp cornflour blended with 3 tbsp chicken stock

Marinade

190mL orange juice

1 tbsp grated orange rind

1/2 tsp French mustard

1/2 tsp ground nutmeg

1/2 tsp curry powder

freshly ground black pepper

1 To make marinade, combine orange juice, rind, mustard, nutmeg and curry powder in a shallow glass dish. Season to taste with pepper. Add chicken and marinate for 1–2 hours.

2 Transfer the chicken and a little of the marinade to a baking dish. Bake for 30 minutes or until chicken is tender. Place remaining marinade and cornflour mixture in a saucepan. Cook over medium heat until sauce boils and thickens. Spoon over chicken and serve.

Serves 4

Oven temperature 180°C, 350°F, Gas 4

Chicken with Prunes

Preparation 25 mins + 1 hr **Cooking** 35 mins **Calories** 166 **Fat** 9g

10 pitted prunes
1/2 cup apple juice
1 kg chicken thigh pieces
1 tbsp olive oil
1 onion, finely chopped
1 green apple, peeled and sliced
salt and pepper
1/4 cup lemon juice
1/4 tsp nutmeg
1 tbsp chopped walnuts

1 Soak prunes in apple juice for 1 hour.

2 Trim the thigh pieces, wash and pat dry.

3 Heat the oil in a deep, lidded frying pan, add thigh pieces and brown well on each side. Remove to a plate.

4 Add onion to the pan and cook until soft. Add apple and cook for 3 minutes, turning once. Season to taste with salt and pepper.

5 Return chicken to the pan, add the prunes and apple juice. Cover and simmer for 25 minutes.

6 When chicken is cooked, remove lid, add lemon juice and nutmeg and cook 5 minutes more.

7 Remove chicken, prunes, apple and sauce to a serving platter. Sprinkle with walnuts and serve with rice and vegetable.

Serves 4

Fish and Shellfish

Bring an air of style and sophistication to your meals with tastes from the deep blue sea. Seafood adds flavours that can't be achieved with meat or poultry. No longer the domain of restaurant menus, people today are bringing cod, salmon, prawns and mussels home to their kitchens as part of a healthy eating regime. Seafood catapults your lunches, brunches and dinners out of the ordinary to ensure you never run out of ideas. Try these recipes out on your family; they're bound to ask for them over and over again.

Chargrilled Tuna with Peach Salsa

Preparation 15 mins + 1 hr standing **Cooking** 3–5 mins **Calories** 332 **Fat** 3g

4 tuna steaks
1 tbsp olive oil
black pepper
chopped fresh coriander to garnish
lime wedges to serve

Salsa

3 ripe peaches, peeled, stoned, and finely chopped
4 spring onions, finely chopped
$1/2$ cup yellow capsicum, deseeded and finely chopped
juice of $1/2$ lime
1 tbsp chopped fresh coriander
black pepper

Salsa

1   Place the peaches, spring onions, capsicum, lime juice, coriander and black pepper in a small bowl and mix well. Cover and set aside for at least 1 hour to let the flavours mingle.

Tuna

1   Preheat the grill to high. Brush the tuna with the oil and season with black pepper. Grill for 3–5 minutes each side, until the fish is cooked and the flesh is beginning to flake. Garnish with the fresh coriander and serve with the lime wedges and peach salsa.

Serves 4

Note: Fresh tuna steaks are a treat on their own, but served with this peach salsa they're absolutely fabulous! The salsa also goes well with ham and pork.

Oven-Baked Cod with Lime and Fresh Herbs

Preparation 10 mins **Cooking** 20 mins **Calories** 175 **Fat** 1g

finely grated zest and juice of 1 lime
juice of ½ lemon
1 tbsp olive oil
1 tsp clear honey
1 tbsp chopped fresh tarragon
1 tbsp chopped fresh parsley
black pepper
4 cod steaks
fresh tarragon and lime slices to garnish

1 Preheat the oven. Place the lime zest and juice, lemon juice, olive oil, honey, tarragon, parsley and pepper in a small bowl and whisk together until thoroughly mixed.

2 Place the cod in an ovenproof dish and pour over the lime mixture. Cover the dish loosely with foil, making sure it doesn't touch the food. Cook for 20 minutes, or until the fish is tender and starting to flake. Garnish with the fresh tarragon and the lime slices.

Note: Honey, citrus juice and tarragon turn baked cod into a really special dish which is incredibly easy to make. Try it with some new potatoes and baby carrots.

Serves 4

Oven temperature 200°C, 400°F, Gas 6

Mussels Marinieres

Preparation 10 mins **Cooking** 10 mins **Calories** 177 **Fat** 2g

1 kg mussels, cleaned
1 small onion, sliced
1 stick of celery, sliced
1 garlic clove, chopped
6 tbsp water or white wine
pepper
1 tbsp butter
1 tbsp parsley, chopped

1 Place mussels, onion, celery, garlic and water or white wine in a large saucepan.

2 Cook over a medium heat until the mussels have opened. Stir frequently to ensure the mussels cook evenly.

3 Add pepper to taste. Stir in the butter and parsley just before serving.

Serves 3–4

Poached Salmon with Asparagus

Preparation 10 mins **Cooking** 5–7 mins **Calories** 403 **Fat** 7g

4 skinless salmon fillets
freshly ground black pepper
¾ cup vegetable stock
¾ cup dry white wine
2 bay leaves
20 asparagus spears
1 tbsp olive oil
snipped fresh chives to garnish
4 lemon wedges to serve

1 Place the salmon in a large, shallow frying pan and season with pepper. Mix together the stock and wine and pour over the fish. Add the bay leaves and cover the pan.

2 Bring to the boil, then reduce the heat and simmer very gently for 10 minutes, or until the fish is cooked and the flesh is just beginning to flake.

3 Meanwhile, preheat the grill to high. Lightly brush the asparagus with the oil and place on the grill rack. Grill for 5–7 minutes, until the asparagus is tender and lightly browned, turning occasionally.

4 Using a fish slice, remove the fish from the stock and place on serving plates with the asparagus. Garnish with a sprinkling of fresh chives and serve with the lemon wedges.

Serves 4

Note: Poaching salmon is really easy and it stops the fish from becoming too dry. You can freeze the leftover stock for up to 2 months and use it for making soups or sauces.

Marinated Fish Kebabs

Preparation 25 mins + 2 hrs marinating **Cooking** 10–15 mins **Calories** 118 **Fat** 2g

4 wooden skewers

1 kg skinless boneless white fish fillet, cut into 2½cm cubes

4 button onions or small spring onions, halved

1 small red and 1 small yellow capsicum, each deseeded and cut into 8 – 12 chunks

1 small zucchini, cut into 12 thin slices

finely grated zest and juice of 1 lemon

2 tbsp freshly squeezed orange juice

1 tbsp dry sherry

2 tsp clear honey

2 cloves garlic, crushed

freshly ground black pepper

fresh herbs, such as rosemary, marjoram and basil, to garnish

1 Soak the skewers in water for 10 minutes while preparing the vegetables. Thread equal amounts of the fish, onions or spring onions, capsicums, and zucchini onto each skewer.

2 Place the kebabs in a shallow non-metallic dish in a single layer. In a small bowl, mix together the lemon zest and juice and the orange juice, sherry, honey, garlic and black pepper, and pour over the kebabs. Turn to coat all over, then cover and refrigerate for 2 hours.

3 Preheat the grill to medium. Grill the kebabs for 10–15 minutes, until the fish is tender, turning occasionally. Baste frequently with the marinade to keep the kebabs moist. Garnish with the fresh herbs.

Serves 4

Seafood and Broccoli Risotto

Preparation 15 mins **Cooking** 10 mins **Calories** 371 **Fat** 6g

1 tbsp sunflower oil

6 spring onions, chopped

1 clove garlic, finely chopped

1 red or yellow capsicum, deseeded and diced

1 cup arborio rice

2 cups vegetable stock

1$\frac{1}{2}$ cups chestnut mushrooms, sliced

1 cup dry white wine

500g frozen seafood selection, defrosted

250g broccoli, cut into small florets

2 tbsp chopped fresh flat-leaf parsley

freshly ground black pepper

1 Heat the oil in a large saucepan, add the spring onions, garlic and capsicum and cook for 5 minutes or until softened, stirring occasionally. Add the rice and cook for 1 minute, stirring, until well coated in the oil.

2 In a separate pan, bring the stock to the boil. Add the mushrooms, wine and $\frac{1}{4}$ cup of the stock to the rice mixture. Bring to a boil, stirring, then simmer, uncovered, for 15 minutes or until most of the liquid is absorbed, stirring often. Add another cup of stock and cook for 15 minutes or until it's absorbed, stirring frequently.

3 Add the seafood and most of the remaining stock and stir frequently for 5 minutes or until the rice is cooked but firm to the bite. Add the rest of the stock, if necessary, and make sure the seafood is cooked through. Meanwhile, cook the broccoli in boiling water for 3 minutes or until tender. Drain well, stir into the risotto with the parsley and season with black pepper.

Serves 4

Note: The secret to cooking a good risotto is to keep adding just enough liquid and to stir as much as possible. You can use any mixture of seafood – prawns and mussels are good.

Vegetable Dishes

The quest for healthy living leaves many people dreading a boring routine of bland vegetables. Well, prepare to banish that belief! Our expert team has summoned all its creative power to bring you these delightful dishes. You'll cultivate a new appreciation of vegetables after exploring each recipe, whether you dig your fork into our spinach soufflé or sink your teeth into our red onion, zucchini, and tomato pizza. Our dishes are fresh, exciting and totally delicious. They're easy to prepare and even easier to eat. The good life never looked or tasted better!

Harvest Vegetable Bake

Preparation 10 mins **Cooking** 1 hr 30 mins **Calories** 154 **Fat** 2g

1 onion, sliced
2 leeks, sliced
2 sticks celery, chopped
2 carrots, thinly sliced
1 red capsicum, deseeded and sliced
500g mixed root vegetables, such as sweet potato, parsnip and turnip, cubed
2 cups mushrooms, sliced
2 cups canned chopped tomatoes
6 tbsp dry cider
1 tsp dried thyme
1 tsp dried oregano
freshly ground black pepper
fresh herbs, such as basil and coriander, to garnish

1 Preheat the oven. Place the onion, leeks, celery, carrots, capsicum, cubed root vegetables and mushrooms in a large ovenproof casserole dish and mix well. Stir in the tomatoes, cider, thyme, oregano, and black pepper.

2 Cover and bake in the centre of the oven for 1–1 $^1\!/_2$ hours, until the vegetables are cooked through and tender, stirring 1–2 times. Garnish with the fresh herbs.

Serves 4

Note: This satisfying vegetable dish is really cheap, especially in Autumn when the ingredients are in season. Serve it with warm crusty bread.

Oven temperature 180°C, 350°F, Gas 4

Bean, Lentil and Eggplant Moussaka

Preparation 30 mins **Cooking** 1 hr **Calories** 370 **Fat** 3g

$^1/_2$ cup continental lentils, rinsed and drained

1 eggplant, thinly sliced

2 tbsp olive oil

2 leeks, sliced

2 sticks celery, chopped

2 cloves garlic, crushed

1 yellow capsicum, deseeded and diced

2 cups canned chopped tomatoes

5 tbsp dry white wine

2 tbsp tomato paste

2 cups canned black-eye beans, drained and rinsed

2 tsp dried mixed herbs

freshly ground black pepper

1$^1/_4$ cups low-fat plain yoghurt

2 medium eggs

2 tbsp finely grated Parmesan cheese

fresh herbs, such as basil, to garnish

1 Add the lentils to a saucepan of boiling water, cover and simmer for 30 minutes or until tender. Drain, rinse, then drain again and set aside.

2 Preheat the oven. Meanwhile, cook the eggplant slices in a saucepan of boiling water for 2 minutes. Drain, pat them dry with kitchen towels and set aside.

3 Heat the oil in a frying pan, add the leeks, celery, garlic and capsicum and cook for 5 minutes or until slightly softened. Add the cooked lentils, tomatoes, wine, tomato paste, beans, mixed herbs and black pepper. Cover and bring to the boil, then simmer for 10 minutes or until the vegetables have softened.

4 Spoon $^1/_2$ the bean and lentil mixture into a shallow ovenproof dish and layer over $^1/_2$ the eggplant. Repeat. Mix together the yoghurt and eggs and pour over the top. Sprinkle over the Parmesan. Cook for 40 minutes or until golden brown and bubbling. Garnish with the fresh herbs.

Serves 4

Note: Plenty of protein here for vegetarians. If you're in a hurry to get supper on the table, you can use canned ready-cooked lentils instead. Serve it with a green salad.

Oven temperature 180°C, 350°F, Gas 4

Stir-Fry Greens

Preparation 5 mins **Cooking** 5 mins **Calories** 70 **Fat** 4g

2 tbsp sesame seeds
1 clove garlic, crushed
200g snow peas
200g Chinese greens such as bok choy,
Chinese broccoli and Chinese
cabbage, chopped
150g bean sprouts
2 tbsp sweet soy sauce
1 tbsp oyster sauce
1 tbsp sweet chilli sauce

1 Place sesame seeds and garlic in a non-stick frying pan and stir-fry over a medium heat for 2 minutes or until golden.

2 Add snow peas, Chinese greens, bean sprouts, soy sauce, oyster sauce and chilli sauce to the pan and stir-fry for 3 minutes or until vegetables are tender. Serve immediately.

Serves 4

Note: Ordinary cabbage is a suitable alternative to the Chinese greens in this recipe.

Spinach Soufflé

Preparation 30 mins **Cooking** 30 mins **Calories** 284 **Fat** 5g

500g fresh spinach

1 tbsp sunflower spread, plus extra for greasing

1 tbsp finely grated Parmesan cheese

1 tbsp plain flour

1 cup low-fat milk

4 medium eggs, separated, plus 1 extra egg white

1/2 cup low-fat finely grated aged Cheddar cheese

freshly ground black pepper

large pinch of ground nutmeg

1 Rinse the spinach, remove any coarse stalks or leaves and place it in a large saucepan. Cover and cook over a low heat for 4–5 minutes or until it has wilted. Drain and squeeze out any excess water. Chop roughly and set aside.

2 Preheat the oven. Grease a 4–cup soufflé dish, sprinkle with Parmesan and set aside. Gently heat the sunflower spread, flour and milk in a pan, whisking continuously, until the sauce boils. Simmer for 3 minutes, stirring. Transfer to a large bowl, add the spinach and mix well. Gradually beat in the egg yolks and $2/3$ of the Cheddar, then season with pepper and nutmeg. Whisk the egg whites in a clean dry bowl until stiff (this is easiest with an electric whisk), then fold into the spinach mixture.

3 Spoon the mixture into the prepared dish and sprinkle with the remaining Cheddar. Bake for 30 minutes or until well risen and lightly set.

Serves 4

Note: To give your soufflé an extra lift, place it on a preheated baking tray just before you put it into the oven.

Oven temperature 190°C, 375°F, Gas 5

Red Onion, Zucchini, and Tomato Pizza

Preparation 25 mins **Cooking** 25–30 mins **Calories** 425 **Fat** 9g

1 tbsp olive oil, plus extra for greasing

2 small red onions, sliced

1 yellow capsicum, deseeded and sliced

2 small zucchini, sliced

1 clove garlic, crushed

2 cups whole-grain flour

2 tsp baking powder

3 tbsp sunflower spread

$^1/_2$ cup low-fat milk

4 tbsp tomato purée

1 tbsp tomato paste

2 tsp dried mixed herbs

freshly ground black pepper

3 small plum tomatoes, sliced

$^1/_2$ cup low-fat aged Cheddar cheese, grated

fresh basil to garnish

1 Preheat the oven. Heat the oil in a saucepan, then add the onions, capsicum, zucchini and garlic and cook for 5 minutes or until softened, stirring occasionally. Set aside.

2 Place the flour and baking powder in a bowl, then rub in the sunflower spread. Stir in the milk to form a smooth dough and knead lightly.

3 Roll the dough out on a lightly floured surface to a circle about 4cm wide and place on a greased baking sheet. Mix together the tomato purée, tomato paste, mixed herbs and black pepper and spread over the dough. Top with the onion mixture.

4 Arrange the tomato slices on top and sprinkle with the Cheddar. Bake for 25–30 minutes, until the cheese is golden brown and bubbling. Garnish with fresh basil.

Serves 4

Note: The red onions start to caramelise and become quite sweet while the pizza is cooking. If you don't have any mixed herbs, use dried oregano or marjoram instead.

Oven temperature 220°C, 425°F, Gas 7

Pumpkin and Artichoke Risotto

Preparation 20 mins **Cooking** 25 mins **Calories** 103 **Fat** 2g

3 cups vegetable stock
1 cup white wine
1 tbsp olive oil
1 onion, chopped
2 tsp ground cumin
$1/2$ tsp nutmeg
200g pumpkin, chopped
330g Arborio or risotto rice
440g canned artichoke hearts, drained and chopped
90g sun-dried tomatoes, chopped
2 tbsp chopped fresh sage
freshly ground black pepper
30g grated Parmesan cheese

1 Place stock and wine in a saucepan and bring to the boil over a medium heat. Reduce heat and keep warm.

2 Heat oil in a saucepan over a medium heat, add onion, cumin and nutmeg and cook, stirring, for 3 minutes or until onion is soft. Add pumpkin and cook, stirring, for 3 minutes.

3 Add rice and cook, stirring, for 5 minutes. Pour 1 cup of hot stock mixture into rice and cook over a medium heat, stirring constantly, until stock is absorbed. Continue cooking in this way until all the stock is used and rice is tender.

4 Add artichokes, sun-dried tomatoes, sage and black pepper to taste to rice mixture. Mix gently and cook for 2 minutes or until heated through. Remove pan from heat, gently stir in Parmesan cheese and serve.

Serves 4

Note: Arborio or risotto rice is traditionally used for making risottos. It absorbs liquid without becoming soft and it is this special quality that makes it so suitable for risottos. A risotto made in the traditional way, where liquid is added gradually as the rice cooks, takes 20–30 minutes to cook.

Desserts

Desserts can remain part of a sensible eating program if they're low in fat and high in taste. We've struck the right balance between the two with our scrumptious sensations, and taken the guilt out of what is sure to be a daily indulgence. Wonderful ingredients such as fruit, yoghurt, honey and figs provide a natural sweetness without tipping the scales, so you can eat them without regret. Take some time to browse through these pages and you'll discover a brand new eating obsession – pleasures for the palate that are good for you, too.

Raspberry Yoghurt Ice

Preparation 15 mins + 6hrs freezing and 30 mins chilling **Calories** 158 **Fat** 1g

3 cups raspberries, defrosted if frozen
$1/4$ cup caster sugar
$1\,1/2$ cups low-fat raspberry yoghurt
$1/2$ cup fat-free plain yoghurt
fresh mint and raspberries to decorate

1 Place the raspberries in a food processor and blend until smooth, or use a hand blender. Press the mixture through a sieve into a bowl, discarding the pips, then add the sugar and mix well.

2 Mix in the raspberry yoghurt and plain yoghurt. Pour the mixture into a shallow freezer container, cover and freeze for 2 hours. Meanwhile, put a large empty bowl into the refrigerator to chill.

3 Spoon the raspberry mixture into the chilled bowl and beat with a fork or whisk until smooth to break down the ice crystals. Return to the container, cover and freeze for a further 4 hours or until firm.

4 Transfer to the fridge for 30 minutes before serving to soften. Serve in scoops, decorated with the fresh mint and raspberries.

Serves 4

Note: The unmistakable flavour of raspberries works really well in this tangy ice, but there's nothing to stop you using fresh strawberries and strawberry yoghurt instead.

Grilled Honeyed Fruit with Vanilla Yoghurt

Preparation 15 mins **Cooking** 10 mins **Calories** 243 **Fat** 5g

3 tbsp clear honey

2 tbsp unsweetened apple juice

1 tsp ground mixed spice

1 ripe mango

1 small pineapple, peeled, cored and sliced

2 eating apples, peeled, cored and sliced

2 pears, peeled, cored and sliced

1 $\frac{1}{4}$ cup low-fat plain yoghurt

few drops of vanilla extract

1 Preheat the grill to high. In a bowl, mix together 2 tablespoons of the honey with the apple juice and mixed spice. Peel the mango and slice the flesh off the stone.

2 Cover the grill rack with foil and lay $\frac{1}{2}$ the mango and the pineapple, apple, and pear slices on it. Drizzle over $\frac{1}{2}$ the honeyed spice mixture. Grill for 10 minutes or until slightly softened, turning the fruit once. Keep it warm while you repeat with the remaining fruit and honey mixture.

3 Meanwhile, place the yoghurt in a bowl with the vanilla extract and the remaining honey, then mix well. Serve the fruit warm with the vanilla yoghurt mixture.

Serves 4–6

Note: Fruit drizzled with honey and grilled until it just starts to brown is wonderful served warm with ice cream. But it's better still with vanilla yoghurt spooned over it.

Boiled Orange, Lime and Almond Cake

Preparation 15 mins + 2 hrs boiling **Cooking** 1 hr **Calories** 410 **Fat** 3g

2 navel oranges and 4 thin skinned limes, (about 350g total weight)

canola cooking spray

3 eggs

4 egg whites

1$\frac{1}{2}$ cups sugar

1 tsp baking powder

2 cups almond meal

reduced fat ice-cream or yoghurt, to serve

1 Scrub the oranges and limes. Put the oranges in a large pot of boiling water and simmer for 1 hour. Add the limes and continue cooking for 1 hour more, or until all the fruit is very soft. Remove from the water and allow to cool. Cut the fruit in $\frac{1}{2}$ remove the seeds, and discard. Put the remaining whole fruit, including the skins, into a blender or food processor and blend until smooth.

2 Preheat the oven. Lightly spray a 23cm springform tin with the canola spray and line it with paper.

3 Beat the eggs, egg whites, sugar, and baking powder until thick and pale, then fold in the almond meal and citrus purée.

4 Spoon the mixture into the prepared pan and bake for 1 hour, or until a skewer comes out clean when inserted in the centre.

5 Allow to cool in the tin. Serve with the reduced fat ice-cream or yoghurt.

Serves 8–10

Oven temperature 190°C, 375°F, Gas 5

Ricotta Torte with Fruit Compote

Preparation 15 mins + 30 mins chilling **Cooking** 10 mins **Calories** 345 each **Fat** 7g each

canola cooking spray
150g reduced fat plain (sweet) biscuits
2 tbsp pecan nuts, toasted
3 tbsp polyunsaturated spread or margarine, melted
1$\frac{1}{2}$ tsp powdered gelatin
zest and juice of 2 small oranges
zest and juice of 2 small lemons
1$\frac{1}{2}$ cups reduced fat ricotta cheese, well drained
$\frac{1}{4}$ cup caster sugar
1 cup reduced fat sour cream
2 eggs, separated

Compote
$\frac{1}{2}$ cup dried figs
$\frac{1}{2}$ cup pitted prunes
$\frac{1}{2}$ cup dried apricots
$\frac{1}{2}$ cup dried cherries
2 tbsp good quality Marsala
$\frac{1}{3}$ cup orange juice
zest of 1 orange

Torte

1. Spray a 20cm springform tin with canola spray and line the base with baking paper. Process the biscuits and nuts to fine crumbs. Add the spread or margarine and process for a few seconds to combine. Press firmly into the base of the tin. Chill for 30 minutes.

2. Dissolve the gelatin in a little hot water. Put the combined juices (but not the zest) in a small pot and heat gently. Add the gelatin. Remove from the heat and stir to dissolve the gelatin.

3. Beat the ricotta, sugar, sour cream, egg yolks and zest with an electric beater, then gradually pour in the gelatin mixture and beat slowly to combine.

4. Whisk the egg whites until stiff peaks form, fold 2–3 tablespoons of the egg whites into the ricotta mixture to lighten, then fold through the remaining whites, trying not to deflate the mix. Pour over the cookie base, cover and chill for at least 30 minutes. Slice into 10 portions.

Compote

1. Put the figs, prunes, apricots and cherries in a bowl and add the Marsala, orange juice and zest. Macerate in the refrigerator overnight. Serve the torte with fruit compote.

Serves 10

Glossary

Acidulated water: water with added acid, such as lemon juice or vinegar, which prevents discolouration of ingredients, particularly fruit or vegetables. The proportion of acid to water is 1 teaspoon per 300mL.

Al dente: Italian cooking term for ingredients that are cooked until tender but still firm to the bite; usually applied to pasta.

Americaine: method of serving seafood, usually lobster and monkfish, in a sauce flavoured with olive oil, aromatic herbs, tomatoes, white wine, fish stock, brandy and tarragon.

Anglaise: cooking style for simple cooked dishes such as boiled vegetables. Assiette anglaise is a plate of cold cooked meats.

Antipasto: Italian for 'before the meal', it denotes an assortment of cold meats, vegetables and cheeses, often marinated, served as an hors d'oeuvre. A typical antipasto might include salami, prosciutto, marinated artichoke hearts, anchovy fillets, olives, tuna fish and Provolone cheese.

Au gratin: food sprinkled with breadcrumbs, often covered with cheese sauce and browned until a crisp coating forms.

Bain marie: a saucepan standing in a large pan which is filled with boiling water to keep liquids at simmering point. A double boiler will do the same job.

Balsamic vinegar: a mild, extremely fragrant, wine-based vinegar made in northern Italy. Traditionally, the vinegar is aged for at least seven years in a series of casks made of various woods.

Baste: to moisten food while it is cooking by spooning or brushing on liquid or fat.

Beat: to stir thoroughly and vigorously.

Beurre manie: equal quantities of butter and flour kneaded together and added, a little at a time, to thicken a stew or casserole.

Bird: see paupiette.

Blanc: a cooking liquid made by adding flour and lemon juice to water in order to keep certain vegetables from discolouring as they cook.

Blanch: to plunge into boiling water and then, in some cases, into cold water. Fruits and nuts are blanched to remove skin easily.

Blanquette: a white stew of lamb, veal or chicken, bound with egg yolks and cream and accompanied by onion and mushrooms.

Blend: to mix thoroughly.

Bonne femme: dishes cooked in the traditional French 'housewife' style. Chicken and pork bonne femme are garnished with bacon, potatoes and baby onion; fish bonne femme with mushrooms in a white wine sauce.

Bouquet garni: a bunch of herbs, usually consisting of sprigs of parsley, thyme, marjoram, rosemary, a bay leaf, peppercorns and cloves, tied in muslin and used to flavour stews and casseroles.

Braise: to cook whole or large pieces of poultry, game, fish, meat or vegetables in a small amount of wine, stock or other liquid in a closed pot. Often the main ingredient is first browned in fat and then cooked in a low oven or very slowly on top of the stove. Braising suits tough meats and older birds and produces a mellow, rich sauce.

Broil: the American term for grilling food.

Brown: cook in a small amount of fat until brown.

Burghul (also bulgur): a type of cracked wheat, where the kernels are steamed and dried before being crushed.

Buttered: to spread with softened or melted butter.

Butterfly: to slit a piece of food in half horizontally, cutting it almost through so that, when opened, it resembles butterfly wings. Chops, large prawns and thick fish fillets are often butterflied so that they cook more quickly.

Buttermilk: a tangy, low-fat cultured milk product; its slight acidity makes it an ideal marinade base for poultry.

Calzone: a semicircular pocket of pizza dough, stuffed with meat or vegetables, sealed and baked.

Caramelise: to melt sugar until it is a golden brown syrup.

Champignons: small mushrooms, usually canned.

Chasseur: French for 'hunter'; a French cooking style in which meat and chicken dishes are cooked with mushrooms, spring onions, white wine and often tomato.

Clarify: to melt butter and drain the oil off the sediment.

Coat: to cover with a thin layer of flour, sugar, nuts, crumbs, poppy or sesame seeds, cinnamon sugar or a few of the ground spices.

Concasser: to chop coarsely, usually tomatoes.

Confit: from the French verb confire, meaning to preserve. Food that is made into a preserve by cooking very slowly and thoroughly until tender. In the case of meat, such as duck or goose, it is cooked in its own fat, and covered with the fat so that the meat does not come into contact with the air. Vegetables such as onions are good in confit.

Consommé: a clear soup usually made from beef.

Coulis: a thin puree, usually of fresh or cooked fruit or vegetables, which is soft enough to pour (couler means 'to run'). A coulis may be rough-textured or very smooth.

Court bouillon: the liquid in which fish, poultry or meat is cooked. It usually consists of water with bay leaf, onion, carrots and salt and freshly ground black pepper to taste. Other additives may include wine, vinegar, stock, garlic or spring (green) onions.

Couscous: cereal processed from semolina into pellets, traditionally steamed and served with meat and vegetables in the classic North African stew of the same name.

Cream: to make soft, smooth and creamy by rubbing with the back of a spoon or by beating with a mixer. Usually applied to fat and sugar.

Cróutons: small toasted or fried cubes of bread.

Cruciferous vegetables: certain members of the mustard, cabbage and turnip families with cross-shaped flowers and strong aromas and flavours.

Crudités: raw vegetables, cut in slices or sticks to nibble plain or with a dipping sauce, or shredded vegetables tossed as salad with a simple dressing.

Cube: to cut into small pieces with six equal sides.

Curdle: to cause milk or sauce to separate into solid and liquid. Example, overcooked egg mixtures.

Daikon radish (also called mooli): a long white Japanese radish.

Dark sesame oil (also called Oriental sesame oil): dark polyunsaturated oil with a low burning point, used for seasoning. Do not replace with lighter sesame oil.

Deglaze: to dissolve congealed cooking juices or glaze on the bottom of a pan by adding a liquid, then scraping and stirring vigorously whilst bringing the liquid to the boil. Juices may be used to make gravy or to add to sauce.

Degrease: to skim grease from the surface of liquid. If possible the liquid should be chilled so the fat solidifies. If not, skim off most of the fat with a large metal spoon, then trail strips of paper towel on the surface of the liquid to remove any remaining globules.

Devilled: a dish or sauce that is highly seasoned with a hot ingredient such as mustard, Worcestershire sauce or cayenne pepper.

Dice: to cut into small cubes.

Dietary fibre: a plant-cell material that is undigested or only partially digested in the human body, but which promotes healthy digestion of other food matter.

Dissolve: mix a dry ingredient with liquid until absorbed.

Dredge: to coat with a dry ingredient, as flour or sugar.

Drizzle: to pour in a fine thread-like stream over a surface.

Dust: to sprinkle or coat lightly with flour or icing sugar.

Dutch oven: a heavy casserole with a lid usually made from cast iron or pottery.

Emulsion: a mixture of two liquids that are not mutually soluble; for example, oil and water.

Entree: in Europe, the 'entry' or hors d'oeuvre; in North America entree means the main course.

Fenugreek: a small, slender annual herb of the pea family. The seeds are spice. Ground fenugreek has a strong maple sweetness, spicy but bitter flavour and an aroma of burnt sugar.

Fillet: special cut of beef, lamb, pork or veal; breast of poultry and game; fish cut off the bone lengthways.

Flake: to break into small pieces with a fork.

Flame: to ignite warmed alcohol over food.

Fold in: a gentle, careful combining of a light or delicate mixture with a heavier mixture, using a metal spoon.

Fricassee: a dish in which poultry, fish or vegetables are bound together with a white or veloute sauce. In Britain and the United States, the name applies to an old-fashioned dish of chicken in a creamy sauce.

Galangal: A member of the ginger family, commonly known as Laos or Siamese ginger. It has a peppery taste with overtones of ginger.

Galette: sweet or savoury mixture shaped as a flat round.

Garnish: to decorate food, usually with something edible.

Gastrique: caramelised sugar deglazed with vinegar and used in fruit-flavoured savoury sauces, in such dishes as duck with orange.

Glaze: a thin coating of beaten egg, syrup or aspic which is brushed over pastry, fruits or cooked meats.

Gluten: a protein in flour that is developed when dough is kneaded, making the dough elastic.

Gratin: a dish cooked in the oven or under the grill so that it develops a brown crust. Breadcrumbs or cheese may be sprinkled on top first. Shallow gratin dishes ensure a maximum area of crust.

Grease: to rub or brush lightly with oil or fat.

Infuse: to immerse herbs, spices or other flavourings in hot liquid to flavour it. Infusion takes from 2–5 minutes depending on the flavouring. The liquid should be very hot but not boiling.

Jardinière: a garnish of garden vegetables, typically carrots, pickling onions, French beans and turnips.

Joint: to cut poultry, game or small animals into serving pieces by dividing at the joint.

Julienne: to cut food into match-like strips.

Lights: lungs of an animal, used in various meat preparations such as pates and faggots.

Line: to cover the inside of a container with paper, to protect or aid in removing mixture.

Knead: to work dough using heel of hand with a pressing motion, while stretching and folding the dough.

Macerate: to soak food in liquid to soften.

Marinade: a seasoned liquid, usually an oil and acid mixture, in which meats or other foods are soaked to soften and give more flavour.

Marinara: Italian 'sailor's style' cooking that does not apply to any particular combination of ingredients. Marinara tomato sauce for pasta is the most familiar.

Marinate: to let food stand in a marinade to season and tenderise.

Mask: to cover cooked food with sauce.

Melt: to heat until liquified.

Mince: to grind into very small pieces.

Mix: to combine ingredients by stirring.

Monounsaturated fats: one of three types of fats found in foods. Are believed not to raise the level of cholesterol in the blood.

Niçoise: a garnish of tomatoes, garlic and black olives; a salad with anchovy, tuna and French beans is typical.

Noisette: small 'nut' of lamb cut from boned loin or rack that is rolled, tied and cut in neat slices. Noisette also means flavoured with hazelnuts, or butter cooked to a nut brown colour.

Non-reactive pan: a cooking pan whose surface does not chemically react with food. Materials used include stainless steel, enamel, glass and some alloys.

Normande: a cooking style for fish, with a garnish of prawn, mussels and mushrooms in a white wine cream sauce; for poultry and meat, a sauce with cream, calvados and apple.

Olive oil: various grades of oil extracted from olives. Extra virgin olive oil has a full, fruity flavour and the lowest acidity. Virgin olive oil is slightly higher in acidity and lighter in flavour. Pure olive oil is a processed blend of olive oils and has the highest acidity and lightest taste.

Panade: a mixture for binding stuffings and dumplings, notably quenelles, often of choux pastry or simply breadcrumbs. A panade may also be made of frangipane, pureed potatoes or rice.

Papillote: to cook food in oiled or buttered greasepoof paper or aluminum foil. Also a decorative frill to cover bone ends of chops and poultry drumsticks.

Parboil: to boil or simmer until part cooked (i.e. cooked further than when blanching).

Pare: to cut away outside covering.

Pate: a paste of meat or seafood used as a spread for toast or crackers.

Paupiette: a thin slice of meat, poultry or fish spread with a savoury stuffing and rolled. In the United States this is also called 'bird' and in Britain an 'olive'.

Peel: to strip away outside covering.

Plump: to soak in liquid or moisten thoroughly until full and round.

Poach: to simmer gently in enough hot liquid to cover, using care to retain shape of food.

Polyunsaturated fat: one of the three types of fats found in food. These exist in large quantities in such vegetable oils as safflower, sunflower, corn and soya bean. These fats lower the level of cholesterol in the blood.

Puree: a smooth paste, usually of vegetables or fruits, made by putting foods through a sieve, food mill or liquefying in a blender or food processor.

Ragout: traditionally a well seasoned, rich stew containing meat, vegetables and wine. Nowadays, a term applied to any stewed mixture.

Ramekins: small oval or round individual baking dishes.

Reconstitute: to put moisture back into dehydrated foods by soaking in liquid.

Reduce: to cook over a very high heat, uncovered, until the liquid is reduced by evaporation.

Refresh: to cool hot food quickly, either under running water or by plunging it into iced water, to stop it cooking. Particularly for vegetables and occasionally for shellfish.

Rice vinegar: mild, fragrant vinegar that is less sweet than cider vinegar and not as harsh as distilled malt vinegar. Japanese rice vinegar is milder than the Chinese variety.

Roulade: a piece of meat, usually pork or veal, that is spread with stuffing, rolled and often braised or poached. A roulade may also be a sweet or savoury mixture that is baked in a Swiss roll tin or paper case, filled with a contrasting filling, and rolled.

Roux: A binding for sauces, made with flour and butter or another fatty substance, to which a hot liquid is added. A roux-based sauce may be white, blond or brown, depending on how the butter has been cooked.

Rubbing-in: a method of incorporating fat into flour, by use of fingertips only. Also incorporates air into mixture.

Safflower oil: the vegetable oil that contains the highest proportion of polyunsaturated fats.

Salsa: a juice derived from the main ingredient being cooked, or a sauce added to a dish to enhance its flavour. In Italy the term is often used for pasta sauces; in Mexico the name usually applies to uncooked sauces served as an accompaniment, especially to corn chips.

Saturated fats: one of the three types of fats found in foods. These exist in large quantities in animal products, coconut and palm oils; they raise the level of cholesterol in the blood. As high cholesterol levels may cause heart disease, saturated fat consumption is recommended to be less than 15 percent of calories provided by the daily diet.

Sauté: to cook or brown in small amount of hot fat.

Scald: to bring just to boiling point, usually for milk. Also to rinse with boiling water.

School prawns: delicious eaten just on their own. Smaller prawn than bay, tiger or king. They have a mild flavour, low oiliness and high moisture content, they make excellent cocktails.

Score: to mark food with cuts, notches or lines to prevent curling or to make food more attractive.

Sear: to brown surface quickly over high heat in hot dish.

Seasoned flour: flour with salt and pepper added.

Sift: to shake a dry, powdered substance through a sieve or sifter to remove any lumps and give lightness.

Simmer: to cook food gently in liquid that bubbles steadily just below boiling point so that the food cooks in even heat without breaking up.

Singe: to quickly flame poultry to remove all traces of feathers after plucking.

Skim: to remove a surface layer (often of impurities and scum) from a liquid with a metal spoon or small ladle.

Slivered: sliced in long, thin pieces, usually refers to nuts, especially almonds.

Soften: example: gelatine – sprinkle over cold water and allow to gel (soften) then dissolve and liquefy.

Souse: to cover food, particularly fish, in wine vinegar and spices and cook slowly; the food is cooled in the same liquid. Sousing gives food a pickled flavour.

Steep: to soak in warm or cold liquid in order to soften food and draw out strong flavours or impurities.

Stir-fry: to cook thin slices of meat and vegetable over a high heat in a small amount of oil, stirring constantly to even cooking in a short time. Traditionally cooked in a wok; however, a heavy-based frying pan may be used.

Stock: a liquid containing flavours, extracts and nutrients of bones, meat, fish or vegetables.

Stud: to adorn with; for example, baked ham studded with whole cloves.

Sugo: an Italian sauce made from the liquid or juice extracted from fruit or meat during cooking.

Sweat: to cook sliced or chopped food, usually vegetables, in a little fat and no liquid over very low heat. Foil is pressed on top so that the food steams in its own juices, usually before being added to other dishes.

Thicken: to make a thin, smooth paste by mixing together arrowroot, cornflour or flour with an equal amount of cold water; stir into hot liquid, cook, stirring until thickened.

Timbale: a creamy mixture of vegetables or meat baked in a mould. French for 'kettledrum'; also denotes a drum-shaped baking dish.

Toss: to gently mix ingredients with two forks or fork and spoon.

total fat: the individual daily intake of all three fats previously described in this glossary. Nutritionists recommend that fats provide no more than 35 percent of the energy in the diet.

Vine leaves: tender, lightly flavoured leaves of the grapevine, used in ethnic cuisine as wrappers for savoury mixtures. As the leaves are usually packed in brine, they should be well rinsed before use.

Whip: to beat rapidly, incorporate air and produce expansion.

Zest: thin outer layer of citrus fruits containing the aromatic citrus oil. It is usually thinly pared with a vegetable peeler, or grated with a zester or grater to separate it from the bitter white pith underneath.

Weights and Measures

Cooking is not an exact science; one does not require finely calibrated scales, pipettes and scientific equipment to cook, yet the conversion to metric measures in some countries and its interpretations must have intimidated many a good cook.

In the recipes weights are given for ingredients such, as meats, fish, poultry and some vegetables, but in normal cooking a few ounces or grams one way or another will not affect the success of your dish.

Although recipes have been tested using the Australian Standard 250mL cup, 20mL tablespoon and 5mL teaspoon, they will work just as well with the US and Canadian 8fl oz cup, or the UK 300mL cup. We have used graduated cup measures in preference to tablespoon measures so that proportions are always the same. Where tablespoon measures have been given, they are not crucial measures, so using the smaller tablespoon of the US or UK will not affect the recipe's success. At least we all agree on the teaspoon size.

For breads, cakes and pastries, the only area which might cause concern is where eggs are used, as proportions will then vary. If working with a 250mL or 300mL cup, use large eggs (65g/2^{1}/4oz), adding a little more liquid to the recipe for 300mL cup measures if it seems necessary. Use the medium-sized eggs (55g/2oz) with 8fl oz cup measure. A graduated set of measuring cups and spoons is recommended, the cups in particular for measuring dry ingredients. Remember to level such ingredients to ensure an accurate quantity.

English Measures

All measurements are similar to Australian with two exceptions: the English cup measures 300mL/10^{1}/2 fl oz, whereas the American and Australian cup measure 250mL/8^{3}/4fl oz. The English tablespoon (the Australian dessertspoon) measures 14.8mL /^{1}/2 fl oz against Australian tablespoon of 20mL/^{3}/4fl oz. The Imperial measurement is 20fl oz to the pint, 40fl oz a quart and 160fl oz one gallon.

American Measures

The American reputed pint is 16fl oz, a quart is equal to 32fl oz and the American gallon, 128fl oz. The American tablespoon is equal to 14.8mL/^{1}/2 fl oz, the teaspoon is 5mL/^{1}/6 fl oz. The cup measure is 250 mL/8^{3}/4 fl oz.

Dry Measures

All the measures are level, so when you have filled a cup or spoon, level it off with the edge of a knife. The scale below is the 'cook's equivalent'; it is not an exact conversion of metric to imperial measurement. To calculate the exact metric equivalent yourself, multiply onces x 28.349523 to obtain grams, or divide 28.349523 grams to obtain onces.

Metric grams (g), kilograms (kg)	Imperial ounces (oz), pound (lb)
15g	^{1}/2oz
20g	^{1}/3oz
30g	1oz
55g	2oz
85g	3oz
115g	4oz/^{1}/4 lb
125g	4^{1}/2oz
140/145g	5oz
170g	6oz
200g	7oz
225g	8oz/^{1}/2 lb
315g	11oz
340g	12oz/^{3}/4 lb
370g	13oz
400g	14oz
425g	15oz
455g	16oz/1 lb
1,000g/1kg	35.3oz/2.2 lb
1.5kg	3.33 lb

Oven Temperatures

The Celsius temperatures given here are not exact; they have been rounded off and are given as a guide only. Follow the manufacturer's temperature guide, relating it to oven description given in the recipe. Remember gas ovens are hottest at the top, electric ovens at the bottom and convection-fan forced ovens are usually even throughout. We included Regulo numbers for gas cookers which may assist. To convert °C to °F multiply °C by 9 and divide by 5 then add 32.

	C°	F°	Gas regulo
Very slow	120	250	1
Slow	150	300	2
Moderately slow	160	325	3
Moderate	180	350	4
Moderately hot	190–200	370–400	5–6
Hot	210–220	410–440	6–7
Very hot	230	450	8
Super hot	250–290	475–500	9–10

Cup Measurements

One cup is equal to the following weights.

	Metric	Imperial
Almonds, flaked	85g	3oz
Almonds, slivered, ground	125g	4½oz
Almonds, kernel	155g	5½oz
Apples, dried, chopped	125g	4½oz
Apricots, dried, chopped	190g	6¾oz
Breadcrumbs, packet	125g	4½oz
Breadcrumbs, soft	55g	2oz
Cheese, grated	115g	4oz
Choc bits	155½g	5oz
Coconut, desiccated	90g	3oz
Cornflakes	30g	1oz
Currants	155½g	5oz
Flour	115g	4oz
Fruit, dried (mixed, sultanas etc)	170g	6 oz
Ginger, crystallised, glace	250g	8oz
Honey, treacle, golden syrup	315g	11oz
Mixed peel	225g	8oz
Nuts, chopped	115g	4oz
Prunes, chopped	225g	8oz
Rice, cooked	155g	5½oz
Rice, uncooked	225g	8oz
Rolled oats	90g	3oz
Sesame seeds	115g	4oz
Shortening (butter, margarine)	225g	8oz
Sugar, brown	155g	5½oz
Sugar, granulated or caster	225g	8oz
Sugar, sifted icing	155g	5½oz
Wheatgerm	60g	2oz

Length

Some of us still have trouble converting imperial length to metric. In this scale, measures have been rounded off to the easiest-to-use and most acceptable figures. To obtain the exact metric equivalent in converting inches to centimetres, multiply inches by 2.54 whereby 1 inch equals 25.4 millimetres and 1 millimetre equals 0.03937 inches.

Cake Dish Sizes

Metric	15cm	18cm	20cm	23cm
Imperial	6in	7in	8in	9in

Loaf Dish Sizes

Metric	23 x 12cm	25 x 8cm	28 x 18cm
Imperial	9 x 5in	10 x 3in	11 x 7in

Liquid Measures

Metric millilitres (mL)	Imperial fluid ounce (fl oz)	Cup and Spoon
5mL	⅙ fl oz	1 teaspoon
20mL	⅔ fl oz	1 tablespoon
30mL	1 fl oz	1 tbsp + 2 tsp
55mL	2 fl oz	
63mL	2¼ fl oz	¼ cup
85mL	3 fl oz	
115mL	4 fl oz	
125mL	4½ fl oz	½ cup
150mL	5¼ fl oz	
188mL	6⅔ fl oz	¾ cup
225mL	8 fl oz	
250mL	8¾ fl oz	1 cup
300mL	10½ fl oz	
370mL	13 fl oz	
400mL	14 fl oz	
438mL	15½ fl oz	1¾ cups
455mL	16 fl oz	
500mL	17½ fl oz	2 cups
570mL	0 fl oz	
1 litre	35.3 fl oz	4 cups

Length Measures

Metric millimetres (mm), centimetres (cm)	Imperial inches (in), feet (ft)
5mm, 0.5cm	¼ in
10mm, 1.0cm	½ in
20mm, 2.0cm	¾ in
2.5cm	1in
5 cm	2in
7½ cm	3in
10cm	4in
12½ cm	5in
15cm	6in
18cm	7in
20cm	8in
23cm	9in
25cm	10in
28cm	11in
30cm	12in, 1 foot

Index